From Contemplation to Action:

Promoting Social Justice Through Children's Literature

Carole S. Rhodes
Professor, Literacy Education
Queens College, City University of New York
Flushing, New York
carole.rhodes@qc.cuny.edu

Lori Berman Wolf
Associate Professor
Adelphi University
Garden City, New York
wolf@adelphi.edu

Jacqueline Darvin
Assistant Professor
Department of Secondary Education
Queens College, City University of New York
Flushing, New York
JDarvin@qc.cuny.edu

ISBN: 978-1-57981-063-4

Published by:
    Cummings & Hathaway Publishers
    395 Atlantic Avenue
    East Rockaway, NY 11518
    1 (800) 344-7579

Printed in the United States of America

10 9 8 7 6 5 4 3 2 1

This book is printed on acid-free paper. ∞

Table of Contents

Foreword

Patrick Shannon

These are hard times:
- The American occupation of Iraq is in its fifth year;
- Unemployment is up, and wages are down;
- Forty-seven million Americans are without health insurance;
- Gasoline is headed for $4 a gallon; and
- Ice caps are melting.

Americans suffer hard times differently:
- African American males are more likely to be in jail than in college;
- The US is building a wall along the Mexican border;
- Women make only seventy-two percent of males' salaries for comparable work;
- Infant mortality rates in Mississippi are over twice as high as those in Cuba; and
- Food banks across the United States report increases in requests for aid.

Hard times surround us. We understand them from our vantage points, making sense of the events of our daily lives through our pasts and our access to information about them. Our experiences, histories, and knowledge are often fragmented and always incomplete. Still we struggle to render our lives comprehensible and to develop theories about why things are the way they are and why we are experiencing them in the way that we do. My 95-year-old mother and 20-year-old son, both of whom worked in food banks nearly 75 years apart, have different theories about why these institutions are straining currently. My mother tempers her current concerns with comparisons with the Great Depression and searches for a new New Deal farm bill. Born during Reagan's last year in office and coming of age during the George W. Bush administration, Tim doubts the possibility that a New Deal sense of public good could be rekindled without rethinking globalization as if people mattered. Both know that people who suffer don't choose hard times.

Children experience hard times too, but without the benefit of broad daily experiences, extensive histories, or sophisticated knowledge. They work from their vantage points, and they struggle to make sense of their lives. In some understandings of childhood, adults think that children should be protected from knowledge concerning hard times. I don't write from *experiencing* hard times, because the US has a high rate of child poverty and does not guarantee children health care, housing or food. The US has a social safety net for children, but a modest one when compared to those supported in other developed countries. These notions of childhood fear children's knowledge, believing that they are not capable of comprehending such issues.

Carole Rhodes, Lori Wolf and Jacqueline Darvin believe that knowledge is power, and they have assembled educators who believe children's literature can help mediate hard times for children and young adults. These contributors offer texts that blur vantage points, encouraging children to take another point of view and providing recent and historical contexts for hard times. They describe literacy practices that children can adapt to negotiate the meanings of texts in their lives. Together, these texts and practices encourage students to develop new theories about hard times and to act on their new knowledge. I can't imagine a more hopeful pedagogy and curriculum.

How this book is organized

We have created a Social Action Organizer to guide you as you read this text. This organizer follows a continuum in which we encourage you to consider issues, read the chapters, hopefully become inspired and/or inspire others and then proceed by taking action.

The purpose of this organizer is to facilitate and encourage you to move from contemplation into action.

We begin each chapter with a section labeled "consider." In this section we ask you to consider some of your thoughts and beliefs prior to reading each chapter. We do so, in recognition of the seminal work of Fenstermacher and Richardson, and we encourage both pre-service and in-service teachers to embark on "a process of thought that ends in an action or an intention to act" (1993).

We embrace both Banks' (1996) beliefs that a critical piece of education is social action and Friere's (1973,1978) recognition of the critical importance of actively resisting and transforming our world. It is in the spirit of these scholars that we offer a model to facilitate reflection and social action for teachers. As you read each chapter, we hope that you move along the continuum towards inspiration and social action. The element of social action can be either on a small level or a large one. In either case, we encourage you to talk with your peers and colleagues and develop plans and strategies for action. Please keep in mind the notion that even a very small pebble, when thrown into a still lake, will make a ripple effect that spreads far. Any change, any enlightenment, any movement is better than none.

CSR, LBW, JD

References

Banks, James A. (1996). The Historical Reconstruction of Knowledge About Race: Implications for Transformative Teaching. Multicultural Education, Transformative Knowledge, and Action. E. James Banks, pp. 64-90. New York: Teachers College Press.

Fenstermacher, G. D., and V. Richardson. 1993. The elicitation and reconstruction of practical arguments in teaching. *Journal of Curriculum Studies* 25 (2) 101-114.

Freire, P. (1973). Pedagogy of the oppressed. New York: Seabury Press.

Freire, P. (1978) Education for criticical consciousness. New York: Seabury Press.

Author Contact Information

Carole S. Rhodes
Professor
Department of Secondary Education
Queens College, City University of New York
Flushing, New York
carole.rhodes@qc.cuny.edu

Lori Berman Wolf
Associate Professor
Adelphi University
Garden City, New York
wolf@adelphi.edu

Jacqueline Darvin
Assistant Professor
Department of Secondary Education
Queens College, City University of New York
Flushing, New York
JDarvin@qc.cuny.edu

Kathy Short
The University of Arizona
College of Education
Tucson, AZ
shortk@u.arizona.edu

Douglas Fisher
Professor of Language & Literacy Education
San Diego State University
San Diego, CA
dfisher@mail.sdsu.edu

Gloria Kauffman
Staff Developer, PYP Coordinator
Clavis International Baccalaureate Primary School
Mt. Ory, Moka, Mauritius
kauffmanglo@yahoo.com

Linda Leonard Lamme
Professor
School of Teaching and Learning
University of Florida
lammel@coe.ufl.edu

Bobbi Kabuto
Assistant Professor
Elementary & Early Childhood Department
Queens College, CUNY
Flushing, New York
bobbi.kabuto@qc.cuny.edu

Susan Lenski
Professor
Portland State University
Portland, Oregon
sjlenski@comcast.net

Renee White Clark
Associate Professor, Literacy
St. Joseph's College
Patchogue, New York
rwhite-clark@sjny.edu

Grace Lappin
Associate Professor, Special Education
Hunter College, City University of New York
New York, New York
glrags@aol.com

Patrick Shannon
Professor
Education
Penn State
pxs15@psu.edu

Kathleen Shannon
Instructor
Literacy
Penn State
kds12@psu.edu

Laura Shannon
Doctoral Student
Genetics
University of Wisconsin
lshannon@wisc.edu

Tim Pat Shannon
Undergraduate
Geography
Schreyer Honors
Penn State
tps5026@psu.edu

Chapter 1

Rejecting the "You-Can't-Handle-the Truth" Curriculum:Using Children's Literature to Promote the Teaching of Social (In)Justice

Dr. Jacqueline Darvin

Consider:

❖ *Why is teaching about issues of social justice a teacher's responsibility?*

❖ *What kinds of classroom activities help produce students that are interested in civil participation and fighting against injustice in their daily lives?*

❖ *Why is children's literature an excellent vehicle for promoting the teaching of social (in)justice?*

The climax of the 1992 film *A Few Good Men* occurs during an explosive courtroom showdown between Col. Nathan R. Jessep, played by actor Jack Nicholson, and Lt. Daniel Kaffee, played by Tom Cruise. In this memorable scene, Kaffee, a Navy lawyer who has never been inside a courtroom before, defends two Marines who have been accused of murdering a third, Private Santiago. Kaffee questions Jessep about the death of the young Marine Santiago, but Jessep is a hostile witness who views himself as a military "untouch-

15

able." He believes that he had every right to issue the "Code Red" on Santiago because Santiago was a "screw up" and threatened the safety of all of the US Marines based in Cuba, as well as that of those at home. Kaffee refuses to back down from Jessep, trying to get him to admit on the stand that he issued the "Code Red" against Santiago. The following exchange occurs:

> Jessep: You want answers?
> Kaffee: I think I'm entitled.
> Jessep: You want answers?
> Kaffee: I want the truth.
> Jessep: You can't handle the truth!

Rejecting the "You-Can't-Handle-the-Truth" Curriculum

This dialogue illustrates a concept that we see in educational contexts daily, the idea that our students "can't handle the truth" when it comes to discussing controversial, uncomfortable, and conflict-laden topics in the classroom. Many American educators believe on some level, perhaps unconsciously at times, that it is part of their responsibility as teachers to *protect* students from the ills of society rather than to unpack and expose them. As a result, they create curricula that are designed around a premise of *protection*, rather than *correction*, a "you can't handle the truth" curriculum.

Several people have written about teachers' tendency to misjudge students' abilities to "handle the truth" and the feelings of powerlessness that result when they are sheltered from learning about and acting upon issues of social justice in the classroom. Tyson (2003) writes "Frequently, teachers underestimate students' ability to read and discuss controversial issues. We overlook the reality that many children and young adults face these very challenges, euphemistically called 'controversial issues,' in their personal lives" (54). McCall (1998) argues that "pervasive violence on television, in video games and in schools touches children's lives almost daily. Over the past several years, intolerance of others who are viewed as 'different' has increased, as have crimes motivated by hatred of another's race, ethnicity, gender or sexual orientation... Children and youth frequently do not believe adults are doing all they can to solve these social problems, and feel powerless to make changes themselves" (130).

In addition to facing large, global social justice issues such as AIDS, poverty, slavery and world hunger, students see and experience issues of social injustice in their own lives and in the lives of those around them every day. Christensen (2000), in her book Reading, Writing, and Rising Up: Teaching about Social Justice and the Power of the Written Word, asks teachers to consider several questions when they design curriculum about social justice. She writes:

> "Kids can be cruel, and their cruelty exacts a price from the victims. People experience acts of injustice daily. Sometimes these injustices occur in the form of an unkind comment about a person's weight, facial features, hair, language, ethnic or racial identity, gender, or religion... We can teach students about Frederick Douglass, Lucretia Mott, John Brown, Rosa Parks and Dolores Huerta – larger than life heroes who struggled to end slavery and injustice – but how do we teach them to stand up for the overweight girl sitting next to them in algebra? How do we get them to accept the gay math teacher down the hall? How do we get them to stop teasing a child who does not speak English as a first language?" (82).

These questions are of particular importance when one considers the skyrocketing rate of school shootings and other violent acts that students have perpetrated on their teachers, fellow classmates, and themselves in the last decade alone.

Is Teaching about Issues of Social Justice a Teacher's Responsibility?

Before we can address questions such as these, teachers must first believe that it is their responsibility to teach about issues that will positively impact society, issues such as tolerance, the equitable and respectful treatment of others, and other aspects of human relationships in a free and democratic society. While some teachers embrace this responsibility wholeheartedly and take proud and active roles in "making students kinder and gentler citizens," others, on the opposite side of the spectrum, view this work as the sole responsibility of parents and family members, *not of teachers*. These are the folks that are quick to say, "It's not my job to teach the kids everything that they should be learning at home. I'm here to teach them to read, write and do math." It is my belief that the majority of teachers fall somewhere along the middle of this continuum. They have a desire to help students become better citizens, but are engaged in daily struggles to find the best ways to go about reaching this difficult goal.

Uttech (1997) writes about this issue of teachers taking responsibility to teach about social justice and the power that teachers have to enact positive societal changes:

> "I truly believe that teachers in general enter the profession because they want to make the world a better place. They are interested in social service. They possess a compassion for human life and a concern for social injustice, and I don't believe they want to contribute to the problems – though some teachers inadvertently do... If we take an active role and learn about our students' sociocultural experiences and prior knowledge and incorporate our findings in our methodologies and curriculum, we validate their lives and become advocates at the classroom level." (178).

Sonia Nieto, a proponent of critical multicultural education whose work is strongly influenced by that of Paolo Freire, argues that teachers who believe in the ideals of teaching to promote social justice begin with their own personal transformation and later branch out to transforming the institutions and communities in which they teach (1999).

Political Issues Influence Curricula and Instruction

Many scholars write about the political issues that influence curricula and instruction. Cochran-Smith (2004), Uttech (1997) and Finn (1999) write about the politics that affect what and how we teach and the tremendous impact that politics has on the educational experiences that our children have in schools. Cochran-Smith (2004) writes "The idea that teaching is a political activity is animated by several basic premises. Schools (and how 'knowledge,' 'curriculum,' 'assessment,' and 'access' are constructed and understood in schools) are not neutral grounds but contested sites where power struggles are played out" (18).

Uttech (1997) discusses curriculum and whose knowledge is valued. She asserts that schools are places where the values of particular kinds of knowledge are evident by the curricular issues that are addressed and privileged. Teachers, then, as "brokers" of cultural capital and knowledge can address issues of social justice simply by presenting certain kinds of materials to students in particular ways. These materials are never neutral, therefore, and must be selected with care if teachers want to "value and expand on, rather then degrade or ignore, their diverse experiences, their knowledge, and their heritage" (161).

Finn (1999) discusses the politics that underlie the teaching of literacy in particular and the differences between teaching practices that lead to what he terms "powerful literacy" verses "functional literacy." He asserts, "My explanation of why literacy is not seen as

19

dangerous among the working people and unemployed of the United States is that we have developed two kinds of education. First, there is empowering education, which leads to powerful literacy, the kind of literacy that leads to positions of power and authority. Second, there is domesticating education, which leads to functional literacy, literacy that makes a person productive and dependable, but not troublesome" (Finn, 1999, ix).

It's Not Just What We Teach, But How We Teach

One theme that runs through many of the respected books that have been written about teaching and social justice is the idea that *what* and *how* we teach has a tremendous influence on the resulting educational experience for students. If teachers want to mold students who will be interested in civil participation and fight against injustice in their daily lives, schools, communities, country and the world, they have to be exposed to texts, activities, teaching techniques, dialogue and other curricular and instructional elements that will promote and encourage this type of interaction and involvement. The You-can't-handle-the-truth curricula will simply not suffice.

Unfortunately, however, there are no easy or scripted ways to go about doing this challenging, messy work in classrooms. Cochran-Smith (2004) purports "There are no recipes, no best practices, no models of teaching that work across differences in schools, communities, cultures, subject matters, purposes, and home-school relationships" (64).

Shultz (2003) contends that "the recent focus on individual achievement and whole-group learning guided by scripted dialogues make it difficult, if not impossible, for teachers to listen and respond to the rhythm and balance of the whole class. Democratic communities depend on dialogue and the honoring of individual voices that may clash as people work together toward identifying common beliefs" (74).

The Essential Element of Dialogue in Teaching for Social Justice

So even though teaching in a way that will promote social justice and democratic ideals in classrooms and communities is extremely complex and trying for teachers, it can be done, as the subsequent chapters in this book demonstrate. One instructional component that is often acknowledged in the literature as being essential to teaching for social justice is dialogue.

For Freire (1970), the way to begin to teach about and for social justice begins with dialogue, and dialogue is vital to the reorganization of the student-teacher relationship that will bring about problem-posing, empowering education.

Ira Shor, a writer who is concerned with critical teaching for social change, believes, as Freire did, that dialogue is vital to empowering education for students. He claims that "Dialogue, then, can be thought of as the threads of communication that bind people together and prepare them for reflective action. Dialogue links people together through discourse and links their moments of reflection into moments of action" (1992, 86).

His beliefs stem from Freire's idea that dialogue and the nature of the ways in which it is fostered and implemented in the classroom plays a strong role in re-establishing a student-teacher relationship that is more democratic. He writes, "The politics of dialogue especially preoccupied Freire. He defined dialogue education as a 'horizontal' relationship where people talk mutually, instead of the teacher talking at students or down to them. In this democratic discourse the lecturing voice of the teacher is kept in check. According to Freire (1970, 1973), didactic lecturing, at the heart of traditional classrooms, is antidialogical, a vertical relationship between unequals, with authority on top and the students below, the authority speaking and the students being filled with official content" (Shor, 1992, 86).

Freire wrote about the transformation that occurs in classrooms when dialogue becomes a privileged pedagogical approach in schools. He asserted that students become critical co-investigators in dialogue with the teacher. The teacher presents the material to the students for their consideration, and re-considers her earlier considerations as the students express their own (1970).

Providing Students with Material for Consideration

One of the best ways to promote dialogue in the classroom is by doing as Freire stated and giving students "material for their consideration." In teaching about issues of social justice and promoting dialogue around these issues, literature provides a multitude of opportunities to do this in countless ways. Christensen (2000) writes, "As teachers, we have daily opportunities to affirm that our students' lives and language are unique and important. We do that in the selections of literature we read, in the history we choose to teach, and we do it by giving legitimacy to our students' lives as a content worthy of study" (102).

When selecting literature that will stimulate dialogue about issues of social justice in the classroom, teachers have several things to consider first about what they choose to read with their students, and secondly about how they choose to read and discuss texts and design corresponding activities. Teachers can acknowledge the importance of an author's work while simultaneously discussing possible flaws within the works. Doing so will model and encourage a critical literacy approach in the classroom.

Luckily, there are many children's books that deal with issues of social justice, and these books are readily available. Children's authors such as Eve Bunting, Lynn Cherry, Aranka Siegel, Walter Dean Myers, Tom Feelings, Patricia Polacco, Lawrence Yep, Sandra Cisneros, Gary Soto and many others have written books that contain themes of social justice surrounding issues such as the Holocaust, racism, war, cultural genocide, environmental issues and others.

Teachers' Avoidance of Discussing Uncomfortable Issues

Unfortunately, although many teachers have these books in their schools and classroom libraries, few feel equipped to teach about the controversial themes that are present in these books. In a conference session that I attended at the 2004 Annual Convention of the National Council of Teachers of English (NCTE) in Indianapolis, Indiana, Gloria Ladson-Billings (2004) gave a presentation about teachers' failure to address pertinent themes in children's books, even when those themes are of central importance to the books. She gave examples of teachers using books such as *The Watsons Go to Birmingham – 1963* by Christopher Paul Curtis and *Nettie's Trip South* by Ann Turner and not discussing the racism issues in the books with students at all.

The teachers she observed reading these books with students chose to focus on literary elements such as setting, characters, plot, etc., but did not discuss racism as a theme of central importance. This avoidance of discussing "uncomfortable issues" on the part of teachers is widespread, regardless of the age of the students with whom teachers work.

Just last night, graduate students who are enrolled in a graduate literacy course that I teach at Queens College of the City University of New York were presenting lessons that they designed for secondary level students involving critical literacy. One of my students designed a lesson using two books, *Native Son* by Richard Wright (1940) and *Richard Wright and the Library Card* by Miller & Christie (1999). As she was presenting the lesson to a group of about twenty teachers of mixed ethnicities, she kept using phrases such as, "I don't want to make it a black/white issue" and "I don't want to make anyone feel uncomfortable." She is an African American woman and was very concerned about discussing the racism in these books with her students. She seemed especially concerned that the white people in the room, including me, did not perceive her lesson as being "too black."

This led to a discussion in which I assured her that what she was doing was great and that in order to do justice to these books and to both her black and white students, she must talk about the racism that Richard Wright experienced and that it is perfectly fine if some of her students are uncomfortable with the conversation. She seemed relieved when I convinced her that the mistreatment that Wright experienced clearly was a "black/white issue" and that if she taught students about the cultural and historical contexts of the books, they would have a deeper understanding of the racism that he experienced. The reticence of this teacher to discuss the issues of social justice in this lesson is not unusual, and it is only through receiving continual support and encouragement in teacher education programs that it will be gradually reduced and hopefully eliminated over time.

Christensen (2000) writes about how she has evolved as a teacher and how she tries to follow Freire and Macedo's (1987) advice regarding teaching children to read the word and the world, "Now I see reading as a chance not only to rediscover the past, but to teach students to 'read' the untold stories in the daily news as well. In literature, as in history, many voices have been silenced – women's, African Americans', Latinos', Native Americans', Asian Americans'. Poetry and other kinds of writing that let students respond on an emotional level to society can be a vehicle to excavate those untold stories" (126).

Bridging Cultural and Linguistic Divides

Nieto, Bode and Cochran-Smith write about the need to discuss uncomfortable topics such as those surrounding issues of social justice, particularly when the teacher and her students are of different ethnicities or cultural backgrounds. Nieto (1999) argues that these discussions are particularly important for white students that may not be accustomed to learning about multiple perspectives of issues such as poverty and racism. She writes, "The case even can be made that multicultural education especially benefits majority-group students, who may develop an unrealistic and overblown view of their place in the world because of the unbalanced and incomplete education they have received in the school curriculum in particular and in the larger society in general" (xviii).

Patty Bode, a white art teacher who works with Latino students writes about her experiences in teaching about social justice issues:

> "Naming my position as a White ally underscored my role in multicultural education and provided me with a forum for dialogue among my students. When my third grade Latino student asks me, 'Ms. Bode, if you are not Latina, why do you care so much about Latino art and culture?' I am able to respond with more self-assurance and certainty. Together my students and I frame a context for Dr. Martin Luther King's words, 'Injustice anywhere is a threat to justice everywhere.'" (Nieto, 1997, 140).

Cochran-Smith (2004) emphasizes that when teachers and students are of different cultural backgrounds, it is important for teachers to not only select literature with which students can connect, but to construct dialogue around these texts in ways that are "culturally and linguistically congruent with those of the students." She asserts, Building on what students bring to school means that student teachers acknowledge, value, and work from the cultural and linguistic resources as well as the interests and knowledge of their students" (Cochran-Smith, 2004, 69).

This is extremely complex on many levels. In order to do this, teachers must become attuned to the students' ways of thinking, questioning, expressing themselves, asking questions, responding to questions, reacting to differing opinions, etc. It is in these subtle behaviors that a teacher can become more comfortable with creating dialogue in her classroom and as this process becomes more natural, address more controversial topics and select texts that will act as catalysts for social action projects. One strategy for uncovering students' "social participation structures" and "narrative and questioning styles" is by providing them with a rich variety of texts to which they can respond verbally and in writing.

Balancing Mirrors and Windows

Daniels and Zemelman (2004) argue for a balance of "mirrors and windows" when presenting literary texts to students. I believe, as they do, that "some of what kids read in school should hold up a mirror to them, by including their story, their culture, their experience. This is a way of saying, you and your family are important, you are part of us, part of our country and culture. But other books should act as windows, where kids look at not their own reflection, but upon other people's, other time periods, other stories, and values, and ways of life" (59).

Once the teacher has found texts (both mirrors and windows) that deal with issues of social justice, provided students with opportunities to write and dialogue about these books without circumventing or eliminating the "uncomfortable discussions" and silences that often accompany the teaching of controversial texts, and offered classroom activities that get students to think and react to societal problems that are of concern to them and their communities, the last and most important phase of using literature to promote social justice involves taking real actions on the part of the students.

Taking Action

McCall (1998) argues "It's time to examine the use of literature as a catalyst for social action. Now that many teachers embrace the use of literature in their classrooms and use many avenues for responding to books, social action can be an important addition to the repertoire of response strategies" (130). Edelsky (1996) also includes the element of action in her urgings of literacy educators. She, like McCall, believes that educators, in addition to incorporating the Freirian element of critical dialogue in the classroom, should emphasize and help to facilitate action, doing things to further a just society. JoBeth Allen and her colleagues even formed a study group called Literacy Education for a Democratic Society (LEADS) in 1995 "to explore the intersection of progressive education and democratic pedagogy" (Allen, 1999, 2). This group still meets to engage in "critique, hope and action" and tries to "understand and practice education for democracy" (Allen, 4).

In response to a recent assignment that I gave to a class of undergraduate math education students at Queens College, I was amazed that the "action component" was consistently the weakest part of the lessons. For this assignment, students were asked to create lessons that integrated literacy and mathematical concepts. These assignments were required to contain the 4 Principles of Critical Literacy by Maureen McLaughlin & Glenn DeVoogd (2004). One of the 4 Principles involves "focusing on issues of power and promoting reflection, transformation and action." Interestingly, although the students did a wonderful job explaining the reflective and transformative aspects of their lessons, very few were able to articulate the action component. Students wrote things in their lesson plans like, "Hopefully this will encourage students to write letters to their Congressman" or "Perhaps this lesson will encourage the students to boycott this company due to its unjust labor policies." They were afraid to include the action component as a required activity in the lesson and instead, left the action component as a "free choice" for the students. Anyone who has taught elementary or secondary school knows that the likelihood of students having the skills or desire to do these things without the help and support of their teacher is slim to none.

Teachers and students who have engaged in projects that begin with dialogue surrounding literature and end with students' taking actions in their schools, communities, states and even countries report feeling tremendously successful as a result of their endeavors. Christensen (2000) wrote about a project in which her high school students wrote stories about gang violence and shared them with young children at their neighborhood elementary school, "The seriousness that the students showed was in sharp contrast to the seeming apathy they had displayed at the year's beginning... We moved from ideas to action, perhaps the most elusive objective in any classroom. Community and activism: These are the goals in every course I teach. The steps we take to reach them are not often in a straight path. We stagger, sidestep, stumble, and then rise to stride ahead again" (9).

Michalove (1999), a fourth grade teacher who used several texts and interviews with family and community members to help her students dialogue about prejudice and discrimination and create a ballet that was performed for the entire school, wrote about her experience:

> "There was a very real difference in the way students treated one another. I noticed; the students noticed; parents even noticed. At parent conferences several weeks later, unsolicited, one black parent and one white parent (whose child had been teased considerably less about his weight since our discussions) told me how much they appreciated the study. They said their children were really more aware of the issues now, and the adults appreciated the opportunity to talk with their children about such concerns at home, to be resources for their child's schoolwork" (31).

Our Students Can Handle the Truth!

I think that the bottom line for teachers today is that our students can handle the truth when it comes to reading about, discussing and acting upon issues of social justice that affect their lives and the lives of those around them. It is imperative that teachers discontinue the "you-can't-handle-the-truth" curricula and focus instead on giving our children the appropriate tools that they will need to foster positive changes in society. In her book *Regarding the Pain of Others*, the late Susan Sontag wrote, "Some people will do anything to keep themselves from being moved" (111). Are those the kind of young citizens that we hope to mold in American classrooms?

According to the A.C. Nielsen Co. (2005), the average American child spends 4 hours each day watching television or 1,680 minutes each week. The number of minutes per week that parents spend in *meaningful conversation* with their children is approximately 3.5. By the time a child finishes elementary school, he or she will have witnessed over 8,000 murders and by age 18, over 200,000 violent acts on television. On television news programs, 53.8 % of the viewing time is devoted to stories about crime, disaster and war, whereas only .7 % is devoted to public service announcements.

What these statistics and others like them show is that American children are, in fact, being exposed to horrible truths each and every day. Unfortunately, however, parents and teachers are not doing all that they can to help children to sort out and make sense of the issues of social injustice that they are exposed to, often leaving children and young adults feeling frightened, anxious, and helpless to do anything to change the negative aspects of society that surround and bombard them daily. Hence, it's not that our kids "can't handle the truth," it's simply that they need the adults around them to support them through the process of trying to understand issues of social (in)justice and help them to feel empowered about their abilities to enact positive changes.

In the memorable courtroom confrontation between Col. Nathan R. Jessep (Jack Nicholson) and Lt. Daniel Kaffee (Tom Cruise) that I referred to at the beginning of this chapter, Jessup tells Kaffee, "You don't want the truth because deep down in places you don't talk about at parties, you want me on that wall, you need me on that wall. We use words like honor, code, loyalty. We use these words as the backbone of a life spent defending something. You use them as a punch line." Students desperately need us teachers to pick up our literary weapons and stand posts in the fights to stamp out social injustices in our schools, communities and countries. It is only then that we are *truly deserving* of the freedoms and privileges that are provided to us as members of a democratic society.

References

Allen, J. (1999). *Class Actions: Teaching for social justice in elementary and middle school.* New York: Teachers College Press.

Cochran-Smith, M. (2004). *Walking the road: Race, diversity, and social justice in teacher education.* New York: Teachers College Press.

Christensen, L. (2000). *Reading, writing, and rising up: Teaching about social justice and the power of the written word.* Milwaukee, WI: Rethinking Schools.

Curtis, C. P. (1995). *The Watsons go to Birmingham – 1963.* New York: Bantum Doubleday Dell Publishing.

Daniels, H. & Zemelman, S. (2004). *Subjects matter: Every teacher's guide to content-area reading.* Portsmouth, NH: Heinemann.

Edelsky, C. (1996). *With literacy and justice for all: Rethinking the social in language and education.* London: Falmer Press.

Finn, P. (1999). *Literacy with an attitude: Educating working-class children in their own self-interest.* Albany, NY: SUNY Press.

Freire, P. (1970). *Pedagogy of the oppressed.* New York: The Continuum Publishing Company.

Freire, P. (1973). *Education for critical consciousness.* New York: Seabury.

Freire, P. & Macedo, D. (1987). *Literacy: Reading the word and the world.* South Hadley, MA: Bergin & Garvey.

Greene, M. (1995). *Releasing the imagination: Essays on education, the arts, and social change.* San Francisco, CA: Jossey-Bass.

Ladson-Billings (2004). Conference presentation at the National Council of Teachers of English (NCTE) Annual Convention in Indianapolis, Indiana, November 18-23, 2004.

McCall, A. (1998). Why not do something? Literature as a catalyst for social action. *Childhood education.* V74(n3), 130-136.

McLaughlin, M. & DeVoogd, G. (2004, September). Critical literacy as comprehension: Expanding reader response. *Journal of adolescent & adult literacy*, 48(1), 52-62.

Michalove, B. (1999). Circling in: Examining prejudice in history and ourselves. In J. Allen (Ed.). *Class Actions: Teaching for social justice in elementary and middle school.* New York: Teachers College Press, pp. 21-33.

Miller, W. (1999). *Richard Wright and the library card.* Lee & Low Books.

Nieto, S. (1999). *The Light in their eyes: Creating multicultural learning communities.* New York: Teacher College Press.

Schultz, K. (2003). *Listening: A framework for teaching across differences.* New York: Teachers College Press.

Shor, I. (1992). *Empowering education: Critical teaching for social change.* Chicago, IL: University of Chicago Press.

Sontag, S. (2003). *Regarding the pain of others.* New York: Farrar, Straus and Giroux.

Sorkin, A. (1992). *A few good men.* (screenplay). Directed by Rob Reiner. Quotes from www.imdb.com.

Nielson Television Statistics (2005): Compiled by TV-Free America , 1322 18th Street, NW Washington, DC 20036 ,(202) 887-4036, http://www.csun.edu/~vceed002/health/docs/tv&health.html#tv_stats

Turner, A. (1987). *Nettie's trip south.* New York: Aladin Paperbacks.

Tyson, C. (2003). Once upon a time: Teaching about women and social justice through literature. *Social education.* V67 (1), 54-58.

Uttech, M. (1997). Vale la pena: Advocacy along the borderlines. In D. Taylor, D. Coughlin & J. Marasco (Eds.). *Teaching and advocacy* (pp. 160-178). York, ME: Stenhouse Publishers.

Wright, R. (1998). *Native son.* New York: Harper Perennial.

Chapter 2

Imagining Our Way into Social Justice

Kathy G. Short and Gloria Kauffman

Consider:

❖ *How can literature and the arts facilitate children's explorations of prejudice?*

❖ *Why is dialogue crucial to facilitating critical literacy in classrooms?*

❖ *What can happen when students take action as a result of their investigations and engagements with literature? What results can occur when they don't take action?*

> *I learned was how to speak out and not be afraid. Today I was having a discussion with Sarah and Tomás. We talked about what prejudice was and how people risked their lives to live. Prejudice is hard to talk about but you get better at it.* (Javier, age 11)

Talking about social justice issues in the classroom is not easy, but children do "get better at it" when they are given that opportunity, and, more importantly, they change the ways in which they think about and act in the world. Education for social justice involves

33

thinking and living in more inclusive and expansive ways through critically reflecting on structures of power and inequality and connecting that reflection to action (Nieto, 2000). Because schools as institutions focus on maintaining the status quo, discussions of power and inequality are rare in most classrooms, especially in the current political context of mandated curriculum, standardization, and high-stakes testing. Schools, however, are also charged with preparing students for active membership in a democracy (Dewey, 1916), and that preparation should go beyond discussions of the American Revolution to the ways in which democracy plays out in our day-to-day lives, including difficult social issues such as prejudice.

Education for social justice involves more than adding lessons on human relations and sensitivity training to the curriculum with the goal of appreciating cultural differences. The goal, instead, is to transform society and to ensure greater voice, power, and equity for marginalized cultures by identifying and acting on issues of inequality, discrimination, and oppression (Banks, 2001). Macedo (2003) argues that a true democracy is based on a form of literacy that enables learners to develop their critical capabilities for self-defense and liberation. As students learn to read the world as well as the word (Freire, 1970), they begin to question the assumptions of institutionalized knowledge and learn to use that knowledge to take action in order to make the world a more just and humane place in which to live.

Understanding and critically reflecting on the world through our own and others' perspectives plays a key role in identifying sociopolitical issues. This ability to imagine our way into others' thinking and experiences can be developed through significant engagements with literature and through dialogue with other readers (Rosenblatt, 1938). We share a long-term interest in exploring how response to literature through multiple sign systems can support children in considering alternative perspectives within their inquiries of social justice issues and in constructing understandings of education as democracy (Short & Kauffman, 2000; Short, Kauffman, & Kahn, 2000; Short, Schroeder, Laird, Kauffman, Ferguson, & Crawford, 1996). Our collaborations allow us to combine Kathy's perspective as a university educator and Gloria's experiences as a classroom teacher to examine children's inquiries into difficult social issues.

The particular inquiry that we share in this chapter grew out of tensions between students in Gloria's multiage fourth/fifth grade classroom that reflected larger tensions within the school and community. Some of these tensions grew out of incidents of prejudice and discrimination between specific ethnic groups in this working-class urban community including Latinos, African Americans, American Indians, Asian Americans, and European Americans. Other tensions were related to issues of gender and social class and to differences in peer status that are often significant for students of this age level. Children were coming into the classroom from lunch and recess upset at the use of racial slurs and other name calling and those tensions were having a negative effect on the classroom learning community.

Because Gloria works to create a community based in democracy and the valuing of both the individual and the group, she wanted to openly address these issues of prejudice with her students. She knew, however, that students needed a safe way to begin talking about these issues before they could address them directly in their interactions with each other. We decided to create initial plans for an inquiry in which students would consider prejudice in the world and in their own lives through responses to literature and the arts.

This chapter tells the story of that inquiry with students and the ways in which literature and the arts facilitated children's explorations of prejudice. This inquiry is framed by our beliefs about the ways in which literature and the arts support democracy within a classroom setting.

The Role of the Imagination within Democracy

Our understandings of democracy are based in the work of Dewey (1916) and Rosenblatt (1938). Dewey believed that democratic social arrangements within classrooms support a higher quality of human experience that is more accessible and enjoyable for learners than traditional methods based in coercion and repression. Dewey saw democracy as based in a negotiation between individual diversity and community needs where each person has the right to his/her own values and opinions but also needs to take into account the consequences of those beliefs for oneself and others. Rosenblatt argued that democracy involves a conviction and enthusiasm about one's own ideas along with an open mind to others' points of views and needs. She believed that imagination, the ability to try on alternative perspectives and ways of thinking about the world, is essential to democracy and is encouraged by literature and dialogue as response to literature. Her theories of reading as a transactional process posit response as both personal connection and group dialogue. Although she argued that students first need to share their initial personal responses and connections, a valuing of individual voice, she viewed personal responses as essential but not sufficient. Students, therefore, need to engage in dialogue with others where they critique their personal responses and consider other perspectives. Freire (1970) characterized this dialogue as wrestling with words, not just walking on the top of words. He believed that dialogue powerfully combines love, humility, faith in others, hope, and critical thinking and so is the tool that has the most potential for transforming society.

This process of dialogue involves negotiation between students as they collaboratively work together at meaning making about a particular text, with the goal of creating and critiquing their understandings, not necessarily coming to the same interpretation. Shannon (1993) highlights negotiation by arguing that democracy is a system in which people participate meaningfully in the decisions that affect

36

their lives. This participation involves negotiation among equals about both the decisions and the determination of the choices that are the focus of those decisions--the behind-the-scenes thinking that teachers often do and impose onto students.

We believe that negotiation and response to literature also relates to children's responses to texts from other sign systems. We define sign systems as all the ways in which human beings share and make meaning, including art, music, dance, drama, mathematics, and language (Peirce, 1966). These sign systems are basic processes of signification which are available to all learners. Since human beings do not have direct access to their world, they cognitively "read" sensory impulses through the mediation of particular cultural perspectives as "signs" to which they assign meaning. From a sign system perspective, a text can be defined as any chunk of meaning that has unity and can be shared with others. A text, therefore, can be a novel, a painting, a sculpture, a play, a dance, or a song. Response is not just talk, but response through various sign systems to different types of texts.

In our classroom inquiry about prejudice, we offered students multiple opportunities to imagine themselves into others' perspectives through their responses to a range of texts (literature, art, drama, and music) and through dialogue that challenged their conceptions of difficult social issues. In particular, we wanted to engage students in transmediation (Eco, 1976), the process of taking understandings created in one sign system and moving them into another sign system in order to challenge and complexify their views of the world.

The process of transmediation is not a simple transfer or translation of meaning from one system to another because the meaning potentials of each system differ. Instead, learners transform their understandings through inventing a connection so that the content of one sign system is mapped onto the expression plane of another (Siegel, 1995). They search for commonalities in meanings across sign systems but, since each system has different meaning potentials and there is no one-to-one correspondence, their search creates anomalies and tension. In turn, the tension encourages learners to invent a way to cross the gap as they move to another sign system and, in so doing, they think more generatively and reflectively. They create a metaphor that allows them to think symbolically, make new connections, ask their own questions, and open new lines of thinking (Siegel, 1995). Transmediation is thus a generative process in which new interpretations are considered and learner's understandings are enhanced.

An Inquiry about Prejudice

Our planning for this classroom focus on prejudice was based in our beliefs about inquiry and our use of the inquiry cycle as a curricular framework (Short & Harste, 1996). We knew that we needed to begin by planning engagements so that children could connect to their own experiences and conceptions. We also needed to offer a range of invitations that would encourage children to expand their perspectives and understandings. Out of these connections and invitations, we believed that compelling tensions would arise for children to pursue in investigations and that opportunities for presenting their new understandings and for taking action would arise out of these investigations. We spent time carefully thinking through the initial experiences, but did not know where the children's inquiries might go.

Figure 1. The Inquiry Cycle

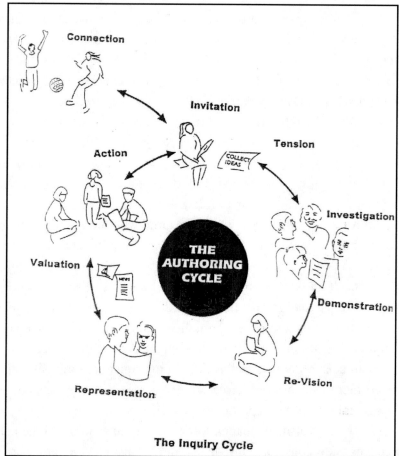

The Inquiry Cycle

Connecting to Children's Current Understandings

We believe that curriculum always begins, not with what we think we should teach children about a particular topic, but with listening to children. The initial engagements should encourage children to think about and share their own experiences. We wanted to listen to their stories and understand their beliefs about prejudice.

We asked children to talk about they thought word "prejudice" meant. In several class discussions, it became apparent that their ideas about

39

prejudice were based on the media and school emphasis on prejudice as racial tensions between blacks and whites. They did not associate prejudice with their own lives, but with issues of history and race, specifically with slavery and with Martin Luther King, Rosa Parks, and the Civil Rights movement. We knew we needed to challenge their limited perceptions which kept prejudice safely outside their own lives.

We asked them to bring in artifacts (objects, photographs, newspaper articles, etc.) that they thought reflected prejudice. The artifacts straggled in, a few each day, and so we began each morning with a sharing time for whomever had remembered to bring an artifact that day. We engaged in a strategy called Save the Last Word for Me (Short & Harste, 1996), where the child who brought the artifact would show it to the class, but say nothing about it. The other class members talked about how they thought that artifact reflected prejudice. The child who brought the artifact remained silent during this discussion, but was given "the last word" to share why he or she had brought that artifact to reflect prejudice. This particular engagement encouraged children to think more deeply about their understandings of prejudice in order to select an artifact to bring to school, but it also forced them to consider alternative perspectives as they listened to class members discuss a particular artifact.

The types of artifacts that children brought to school and the perspectives they considered gradually moved beyond prejudice as a historical problem between blacks and whites. For example, Lupita brought a Barbie doll with a chewed off leg as her artifact. As the class discussed her artifact, they realized that almost all of the dolls they saw in stores and catalogs were white and that none of them had ever seen a Latina doll. The nearness of the Christmas holidays clearly influenced their awareness of the toys available to them, and this awareness led them to talk about prejudice as related to the visual images in toys and advertisements that consistently do not reflect their own identities and the decisions of manufacturers about who matters in our society. Lupita's last word raised another type of prejudice when she shared that she brought the doll because it made her think of prejudice toward those with physical disabilities, thus expanding even further what the children considered prejudice.

The children became so interested in the different ways in which prejudice surrounds them in the community and in the world that they decided to create a museum on prejudice. A counter space and bulletin board were cleared for children to place and label their artifacts. The artifacts were quite diverse, ranging from a sports article on the Washington Redskins reflecting prejudice toward American Indians to a basketball reflecting the exclusion of girls from boys' games at recess. They continued to add new perspectives on prejudice to this museum throughout our inquiry, even after the class moved on to other engagements.

Inviting New Perspectives and Understandings

These initial engagements with inquiry encouraged children to think about their own connections to prejudice and to build from those connections to consider new perspectives. We wanted to challenge and expand their perspectives and understandings to a greater extent through a range of engagements involving responses to literature and other sign system texts.

We read aloud picture books to the class and discussed the different ways in which prejudice is part of our lives and society. We carefully chose books that would broaden the issues of prejudice that children were considering and that had powerful visual images as well as written text, such as *Be Good to Eddie Lee* (Fleming, 1993), *The Giantess* (Hasler, 1997), *Ba-Nam* (Lee, 1987), *Baseball Saved Us* (Mochizuki, 1993), *Friends from the Other Side/Amigos del otro lado* (Anzaldua, 1993), *No Mirrors in My Nana's House* (Barnwell, 1998), *Piggybook* (Brown, 1989), and *Just One Flick of a Finger* (Lorbiecki, 1996).

Children's responses to these books indicated their ability to identify multiple forms of prejudice within a piece of literature. *Baseball Saved Us* (Mochizuki, 1993) focuses on a young Japanese American boy in an internment camp during World War II and how he deals with prejudice through playing baseball, both within the camp and later in an elementary school where he is the only Japanese American. Students talked about his experiences of discrimination:

> Antonio: He is lonely because of the discrimination he is experiencing because of his ethnicity.
> Sean: This kid's lonely and he takes all his anger out on the ball.
> Yolanda: Yeah, he was just so frustrated and he knew he had to hit to prove to everybody.
> Antonio: I don't think he was trying to prove he could hit it. He was just trying to show people that he's still a person even though he's different. Look at him here. He looks brave.

Within the same book, they also examined gender issues:

> Ashley: It looks like all the women are the only ones that are doing sewing
> Ramon: Men do some of that.
> Chela: It's stereotyping.
> Ashley: Yeah. You can see all the men out here making the baseball stands and all the women are sewing uniforms.

Their responses to these books also indicated their ability to stand back and question societal assumptions about who they would become. They realized that their decisions would affect their future possibilities, although they saw these decisions as personal ones and did not explore how their decisions and futures were constrained by structural inequalities.

Figure 2. Sketch to Stretch responses to Just One Flick of a Finger (Lorbiecki, 1996).

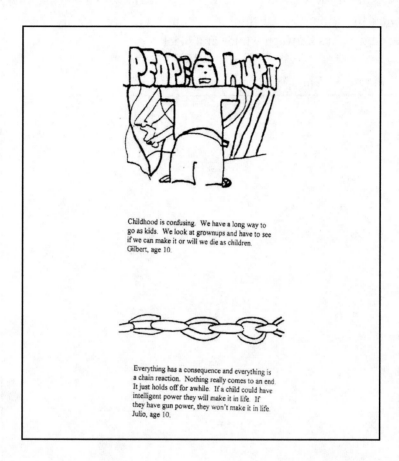

We spent a week reading and discussing several books each day with children. In these discussions, children made a range of connections to prejudice, stating that prejudice is:

- suspicion and not believing in someone
- calling names because someone looks different
- not trusting and assuming someone is not good
- showing disrespect
- excluding someone from the group

At the end of the week, we brainstormed a class web about their conceptions of prejudice. Figure 3 indicates how far the children had come from their initial thinking about prejudice as only involving racial tensions between whites and blacks.

Figure 3. Class Web on Prejudice.

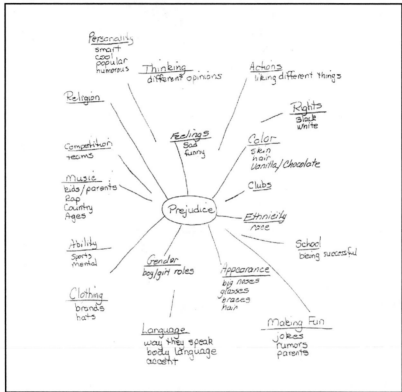

As we examined the web, we realized that their focus was still primarily on the different types of prejudice. We wanted to expand their perspectives beyond who is the target of prejudice to understand the causes of prejudice, the different ways in which people and society manifest prejudice, and the feelings and experiences of those who engage in and are the target of prejudice. We knew that literature and the arts would be particularly significant in these explorations of actions, thinking, and emotions and began gathering resources for a range of engagements. We consulted with the educational coordinator of the photography museum at the university to identify historical and contemporary photographs related to prejudice. We used our own knowledge as well as consulted with art and music educators in the school district's central resource center to gather reproductions of paintings and pieces of music, such as Landscapes by Elinor Coen, various art pieces by Jacob Lawrence and William Johnson, a collection of liberation songs, and the sound track from the movie, Amistad. We also drew from our previous work with reflective drama (O'Neill & Lambert, 1990) to create several drama experiences.

These resources were used within a range of engagements, including:

- Viewing slides of historical photographs reflecting prejudice and hope while listening to music. After several viewings, quiet sketching and writing, and discussions of these photographs with others, Polaroid cameras were made available so children could take their own photographs of prejudice in their community to add to our museum of prejudice.
- Viewing various art prints and sharing initial reactions to how these prints reflect prejudice. Children met in small groups to discuss their thinking about prejudice in response to a particular art print.
- Listening to various pieces of music and responding to that music through Sketch to Stretch (Short & Harste, 1996). Children created sketches about the meaning of that music for them in relation to prejudice.
- Browsing sets of picture books about different aspects of prejudice and responding to those sets on large sheets of paper to create Graffiti Boards (Short & Harste, 1996) where children quickly

jotted and sketched visual images and key words/phrases about the ideas and connections that these books raised for them about prejudice.

The children were given opportunities to think about their responses to the feelings and ideas from these various experiences with books, art pieces, music, and drama through poetry, sketches, quick writes, discussion, and movement. Their responses reflected their move to thinking about prejudice from a broader range of perspectives, and their ability to take more critical stances. Figure 4 provides several examples of sketch to stretches that children created during several of these engagements.

Figure 4. Sketch to Stretch responses to sign system texts about prejudice.

Engaging in Investigations

These engagements with literature and the arts and with responding to these texts through various sign systems led to a growing interest by children in human rights. They saw prejudice as violating the rights of human beings to live with freedom and dignity and were passionate in examining the connections between prejudice and human rights. These concerns led to several class meetings where we listed the issues that children wanted to investigate in greater depth and the children broke into small groups based on common interests. One group wanted to look at the ways in which African Americans experience prejudice in modern society because they had previously assumed that prejudice only happened to African Americans long ago. Another group wanted to look at women and girls and gender roles and stereotypes. A third group wanted to focus on American Indians today, particularly tribal nations in Arizona, because they felt that much of what they found in books was about long ago. A fourth group wanted to focus on children, particularly on the rights of children in relation to the significant adults in their lives, such as their parents. The fifth group focused on the rights of animals and the ways in which people think about and treat animals.

The children decided that they wanted to start with discussing a novel related to their focus as a way for them to form a community through dialogue and to develop some shared understandings and tensions for further research. Literature circles, small group discussions of novels, were a common practice in their classroom and so their choice of these discussions was a way to create a thoughtful and safe environment for them to pursue difficult issues together. For example, the animal rights group read and discussed *Shiloh* (Naylor, 1991), the story of a boy who disobeys his family when he steals and tries to save an abused dog, and the children's rights group read and discussed *Running Out of Time* (Haddix, 1995), a novel in which parents have chosen a particular lifestyle but have hidden the true nature of their community from their children.

The group looking at girls and gender stereotypes read *Just Ella* (Haddix, 1996), a Cinderella story that focuses on what happens after Ella's dream seems to come true when she meets her "Prince Charming" and goes to live in the castle to be trained as the future queen. Ella quickly realizes that she was chosen only for her beauty and that Prince Charming's handsome face hides a vacant soul. Her life becomes a meaningless schedule of protocol and of others telling her who she is and what she must do. The children focused on Ella's struggle to retain who she is on the inside even though others control her every action:

> Talana: She doesn't want to be a princess but she doesn't know who to tell to get out of the situation, so she is stuck in her mind.
>
> Megan: Prince Charming doesn't know what to do. He hasn't had anyone say no to him. She does and he doesn't know how to think for himself or react. He was raised as a prince not to make a decision.
>
> Sanela: She was caught and felt she made a wrong decision. She felt the same outside as inside.
>
> Talana: She tried to only be herself. She is trying to change because they want her. But she doesn't change on the inside.
>
> Donovan: This is better than a fairy tale. She actually changes her life and really cares for people. The prince still lived in the fairy tale.
>
> Carlos: She was still a slave with the prince, just like when she was with her stepmother.

This group went on to create a sketch to stretch that reflected this process of decision-making about whether or not to accept the expectations of others for how girls should think and act. They saw this book as relating to how girls struggle to create their own identities instead of just accepting the identities that others have constructed for them. As they shared this sketch, Talana said, "When girls take risks, they learn to believe in themselves and not give up. They start having rights and they learn to change the world. With a little trust and belief, girls can do anything."

Figure 5. The Identity Hallway.

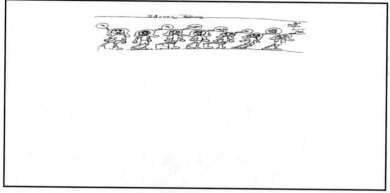

The students who were in the children's rights group were able to move to a broader level of critique in their responses to *Running Out of Time*. They began their discussions with personal stories about the ways in which they felt that their parents and teachers controlled their lives, but gradually moved from these personal responses to critiques of broader power relationships. They created sketch to stretches that reflected their thinking about taking informed action in their lives.

Figure 6. Sketch to Stretch responses to *Running Out of Time* (Haddix, 1995).

This is about having confidence in yourself. It is about what matters inside of yourself. Children are taking a stand and showing who they are. Meagen, Age 10.

Children are learning to speak their mind. They are learning about others. There are walls in our lives that we must climb. We climb over hardships to reach our goals. Ramon, age 10.

Through their discussions, children moved into dialogue where they engaged in critical inquiry together about issues that emerged from the characters' actions within their novels. As they completed their discussions, they identified the issues related to these rights that they wanted to investigate in their own setting. For example, the children investigating the experience of African Americans today interviewed several African American teachers and their principal as part of their inquiry. Each group found a way to investigate their issues through a range of research strategies and then presented what they had learned to the other groups through murals, charts, dramatic skits, and poetry. Each group had to decide what was most significant about what they had learned through their research and then find a sign system that would allow them to powerfully communicate those insights to others in their classroom.

Taking Action

The presentations of their research, in turn, led to class discussions about what they had learned about prejudice and the kinds of action they wanted to take at school or home. We saw this discussion as essential to connecting what they explore in school contexts to their actual lived lives. As Barnes (1976) points out, children often separate their school knowledge from their action knowledge and assume that neither informs the other. We wanted to break down this dichotomy, particularly in relation to social justice issues. Christensen (2000) points out that discussions of social justice issues that do not move to action leave students feeling guilty and/or angry but without a sense of empowerment in working toward change. Banks (2003) agrees, arguing that critique without hope can leave students feeling disillusioned and without agency. As student learn how to critique injustice, they also need to be taught how to create possibilities for taking action to change those injustices.

In this case, one of the results of this discussion was the establishment of new classroom processes and structures for responding to problems between students that involved a committee of students to whom other students could bring problems for discussion, listen to the perspectives of those involved, and create options for solving the problem. The final solution was then negotiated between the students and Gloria, as their classroom teacher. The children decided to call this committee of rotating students, the Democracy Committee, because they saw it as reflecting their right to be part of decision-making processes in the classroom.

Implications for Teaching

One of the many possibilities for literature in the classroom is to serve as the basis for creating tension and challenging students to engage in observation, reflection, theorization, and articulation of difficult social justice issues. Dewey (1938) argues that tension drives the learning process in a generative cycle of action and reflection, leading to new tensions that, in turn, result in more purposeful action and further reflection. Tension is what keeps students alert, monitoring possibilities, taking new risks, stretching themselves and their capabilities. This tension encourages learners to establish a macro view of their efforts and to see mental distance in order to gain a broader perspective and to consider the bigger picture. Because tension acts to maintain students' perspectives, it also encourages them to take a reflective stance on their learning and to develop broader frames of reference and abstractions about issues of social justice that can be used in future experiences.

Creating Tension within a Democratic Classroom

We value the ways in which literature, dialogue, and transmediations across sign systems provide children with the opportunity to analyze and critique the everyday, to question the taken-for-granted aspects of their lives and world. We want children to realize that their use of sign systems position them as participants in a particular culture; that with signs come particular attitudes and assumptions about power and privilege that are often invisible and taken as "common sense" knowledge by insiders within that culture. We shared a range of ideas in this chapter for how children might use literature and the arts to critique these assumptions and to imagine other possibilities, thus opening space to reposition themselves in the world.

Taking Action within a Democratic Classroom

There are many possibilities for students to take action as a result of their investigations and engagements with literature.

Teaching Ideas:

- ❖ Gather and share artifacts to encourage children to share stories of their experiences and to reflect on their initial understandings of a difficult social issue.

- ❖ Encourage multiple interpretations of these understandings through Save the Last Word for Me and the construction of museum displays.

- ❖ Introduce diverse perspectives through picture book text sets and collections of photographs, paintings, and music.

- ❖ Invite students to engage in reflection, inquiry, and critique of these perspectives by responding to these texts through discussion, writing, sketching, webbing, etc. These response engagements should involve students in using multiple sign systems such as art, music and drama in addition to language to share personal connections and experiences and then move to dialogue around critical issues.

- ❖ Invite students to consider alternative points of view through drama engagements, such as tableau and improvisational skits.

- ❖ Investigate tensions that arise from these invitations through small group inquiries that involve both literature circles and in-depth research.

- ❖ Present their investigations to class members in order to consider more complex understandings of the social issues.

- ❖ Make decisions about possibilities for taking action, either individually or as a group or class, in relation to the issues that have arisen out of their investigations

These possibilities should engage students in continuing their thoughtful considerations of the issued as well as considering their own capabilities within their social context. Not taking action can leave students feeling guilty, angry or powerless but taking action in superficial ways is even more problematic in creating misunderstandings about the difficulty of responding to social justice issues. Therefore, instead of developing a list of projects to hand to students, we focused on developing a process of thinking to facilitate students' decision-making.

Teaching Ideas:

❖ Web the most significant understandings they gained from their investigations after presenting their research. Ask "What do we think is most significant out of all the information, ideas, and issues we examined in our investigations?"

❖ Brainstorm a list of the ways in which they could individually or as group or class take action on these new understandings. Ask "So what? Now that we know this, what difference does it make for me and for others around me? What can we do?" What changes can we make in our lives or in sharing with others?

❖ Consider ways of taking action in changing beliefs as well as practices. Ask "How does knowing this affect how I/we think as well as how I/we act? How do I/we think differently?

❖ Engage in discussion and consensus-making to come to a decision about possible action, considering what is actually possible given their age and context and what they are most passionate about doing. Asking, "What seems most reasonable and appropriate from these options for us to do in taking action? What do we most care about?

❖ Consider whether these actions could make a difference for students and others, or if it's being done for the sake of guilt, obligation, attention, or prestige. Asking, "Does this action really have the possibility of making a difference for me and others?"

❖ Make a commitment to an option(s) they will take action on at this moment in time based on these considerations. Ask "What will we commit to doing right now?"

❖ Create a plan for carrying out that action. Ask "How will we go about engaging in this action? What is our plan?"

❖ Carry out the action and then reflect on the consequences of that action. Asking, "What were the results of our plan? What else do we need to do? How do we sustain this action?"The repositioning and critique that is made possible through these ways of taking action are essential to democracy as a "system in which people participate meaningfully without system-derived privilege or prejudice in decisions that affect their lives" (Edelsky, 1994, p. 253). In fact, if we teach students to be literate, but do not also help them develop the ability to critique and act on structural inequalities, we work against democracy and create a threat to justice (Banks, 2003).

Responding to literature provides a way for children to slow down their experiences in the world, to create tension in learning, to support reflection, and to encourage a critical re-theorization of the possible. We believe that this critical theorizing and re-theorizing of everyday experiences and of the possible are essential to creating the critical imagination that is at the heart of democracy. Literature can play a key role in creating classrooms that educate for social justice and democracy--for bringing an end to the oppression of privilege and prejudice and for creating an environment in which people have a significant say in the decisions that affect their lives.

Resources

Anzaldua, G. (1993). *Friends from the other side/Amigos del otro lado*, Ill. C. Mendez. San Francisco: Children's Book Press

Barnwell, Y. (1998). *No mirrors in my nana's house*. Ill. S. S. James. New York: Harcourt Brace.

Browne, A. (1989). *Piggybook*. Boston: Little Brown

Fleming, V. (1993). *Be good to Eddie Lee*. Ill. F. Cooper. New York: Philomel.

Haddix, M. P. (1995) *Running out of time*. New York: Simon and Schuster.

Haddix, M. P. (1996). *Just Ella*. New York: Simon and Schuster.

Hasler, E. (1997). *The giantess*. Ill. .R. Seelig. LaJolla, CA: Kane/ Miller.

Lee, J. (1987) *Ba-Nam*. New York: Henry Holt.

Lorbiecki, M. (1996). *Just one flick of a finger*. Ill. D. Diaz. New York: Dial.

Mochizuki, K. (1993). *Baseball saved us*. New York: Lee & Low.

Naylor, P. (1991). *Shiloh*. New York: Scott Foresman

References

Banks, J. (2001). *Cultural diversity and education*, 4th Edition. Boston: Allyn and Bacon.

Banks, J. (2003). Teaching literacy for social justice and global citizenship. *Language Arts*, 81(1), 18-19.

Barnes, D. (1976). *From communication to curriculum*. London: Penguin.

Christensen, L. (2000). *Reading, writing, and rising up: Teaching about social justice and the power of the written word*. Milwaukee, WI: Rethinking Schools.

Dewey, J. (1916). *Democracy and education*. New York: Macmillan.

Dewey, J. (1938). *Experience and education.* New York: Macmillan.

Eco, U. (1976). *A theory of semiotics.* Bloomington, IN: Indiana University Press.

Edelsky, C. (1994). Education for democracy. *Language Arts,* 71, 252-257.

Eisner, E. (1994). *Cognition and curriculum reconsidered.* New York: Teachers College Press.

Eisner, E. (2002). *The arts and the creation of mind.* New Haven, CN: Yale University Press.

Freire, P. (1970). *Pedagogy of the oppressed.* New York: Continuum.

Harste, J. (2000). Six points of departure. In B. Berghoff, K. Egawa, J. Harste, & B. Hoonan, *Beyond reading and writing: Inquiry, curriculum and multiple ways of knowing.* Urbana, IL: National Council of Teachers of English.

Macedo, D. (2003). Literacy matters. *Language Arts,* 81(1), 12-13.

Nieto, S. (2002). *Language, culture, and teaching.* Mahwah, NJ: Lawrence Erlbaum

O'Neill, C. & Lambert, A. (1990). *Drama structures.* Portsmouth, NH: Heinemann.

Pierce, C. S. (1966). *Collected papers.* Cambridge, MA: Harvard University Press.

Rosenblatt, L. (1938). *Literature as exploration.* Chicago: Modern Language Association.

Shannon, P. (1993). Developing democratic voices. *The Reading Teacher,* 47, 86-94.

Short, K. & Harste, J. (1996). *Creating classrooms for authors and inquirers.* Portsmouth, NH: Heinemann.

Short, K.G. & Kauffman, G. (2000). Exploring sign systems within an inquiry curriculum. In M. Gallego & S. Hollingsworth, eds., *What counts as literacy: Challenging the school stan-*

dard (pp.42-61) New York: Teachers College Press.

Short, K. G., Kauffman, G., Kahn, L. (2000). "I just *need* to draw": Responding to literature across multiple sign systems. *The Reading Teacher*, 54(2): 160-171.

Short, K. G., Schroeder, J., Laird, J., Kauffman, G., Ferguson, M., & Crawford, K.M. (1996). *Learning together through inquiry: From Columbus to integrated curriculum.* York, ME: Stenhouse.

Siegel, M. (1995). More than words: The generative power of transmediation for learning. *Canadian Journal of Education*, 20, 455-475.

Chapter 3

Understanding Yourself Through Literature: Lessons From Adolescents

Douglas Fisher & Maria Grant

Consider:

* ❖ *What do you know about adolescence?*
* ❖ *What problems may arise and how does social justice play a role?*
* ❖ *Why is this such a time of turmoil for many children?*
* ❖ *What can teachers do to help their students during this time in their lives?*
* ❖ *What are some of the reasons that put adolescents at risk for suicide?*
* ❖ *What does this have to do with the curriculum that you teach?*

Anthone and the Terrible, No Good, Very Bad Day in English

"Do we gotta do English today?" Anthone asked his teacher. She responded politely that, yes, they would be "doin' English." Anthone continued to complain about the text the class was reading, *Romeo and Juliet*. "Why he [Romeo] gotta be like that? What's he saying?

59

Man, this sucks." The teacher continued on with the play, reading aloud with expression and passion. Anthone, however, was non-plused. He was not ready to fall into this book nor was he captivated by the ideas presented in the text thus far. As a result, he began to mildly misbehave. His teacher paused and asked, "Why do you think we're reading this book? Aren't you interested in two people who wanted to be together even though their parents wanted them apart? Did you know that one of them will commit suicide as a result? Can you imagine a more important story?"

As Darvin writes in the first chapter, we believe that literature provides readers with both a *window* into places they might never get to see as well as a *mirror* to better see themselves. As Bishop (1994) suggests, the importance of literature is that "serves as a window onto lives and experiences different from their own, and ... as a mirror reflecting themselves and their cultural values, attitudes, and behaviors" (p. xiv).

Teaching Idea:

❖ Ask your students about the issues that are on their minds.
  Ask them for the big ideas that they'd like to read more about.
  Discuss the ways in which they can learn about themselves
  and others through the books they choose to read.

In this chapter, we're interested in the mirror function. We want to explore the ways in which literature can be used to help adolescents learn about themselves and to address the big issues in their lives. While there are any numbers of topics that meet these criteria, our experience in high schools suggests that there are some key issues that are under-addressed in most secondary schools. These issues are often on the minds of adolescent learners and relate to the theme of this book – (in)justice. The remainder of this chapter will present a rationale for addressing each of the issues as well as provide a representative sample of books on the topic.

Relationship Violence

Jessica sat before her teacher (Doug) with a bruise on her left arm. All period, I wondered how it got there. I couldn't imagine that it was "an accident" as she had said when she entered the classroom. I decided to pull her from her class the next period and walk with her to the health center. I assumed that Jessica was the victim of child abuse and I was determined to report it and have her removed from her family. To my surprise, when confronted by the nurse, Jessica confessed that her boyfriend had hit her because she was late to meet him after school. I asked the nurse if this was a problem and was shocked to learn that reports of dating or relationship violence were increasing. Current estimates are that one in every 10 high school girls has been the victim of dating or relationship violence (Flowers, 2002; Howard & Wang, 2003). Most victims are likely to be involved in other violent behaviors, report extreme sadness and suicidal actions, use drugs and alcohol, and engage in high-risk sexual behaviors. Further, according to this study, girls who were black or Latina were at increased risk.

Teaching Idea:

* ❖ Have students write about bullies in their lives – at home and at school. Talk about bullying in their relationships. Males tend to bully more with physical and females more with emotional bullying behaviors. Research together, as a class, some solutions that adolescents can use against bullying.

I was shocked that I didn't know this. I can't imagine the number of adolescent girls (and perhaps boys) who had victims of dating or relationship violence while in my classes. How many teachers knew this, I wondered. I asked around and to my surprise, not one of my

English teacher colleagues knew that this was a significant issue for students. We knew that our students lived with violence all around them (e.g., Fisher, Obidah, Pelton, & Campana, 2005), but hadn't considered that they might be in relationships in which they were being hurt. As we talked, we realized that by not discussing this issue and not making the issue real in school and interrupting it, we were allowing the violence to continue.

It occurred to me that the response to violence was to ensure social justice. Researchers and activists are beginning to conceptualize violence against women as a social justice issue insofar as sexism perpetuates the inequalities that allow violence to take place (e.g., Funk & Berkowitz, 2000). Sleeter (1996), for example, discusses how teachers (and students) integrate information about race, class, gender, and social justice into their existing knowledge base. I knew that needed to address this most horrific form of social injustice.

Teaching Idea:

❖ Bring in a speaker – a survivor of domestic violence. Or a speaker from a women's shelter talking about relationship violence and the cycle of escalation in abusive relationships.

In response, I chose to read aloud *Breathing Underwater* (Flinn, 2001) to the class. The book was recommended by our school librarian as an example of dating violence and how people do and do not deal with it. In one of the daily journal responses, Janae wrote, "You know he loves you. You do things to piss him off, but he loves you. It's not easy to walk away. He could start rumors and ruin you. It's easier to stay."

In response, I wrote back, "Is this you or your response to Caitlin? Let's talk in person. I'm here for you if you need me." Janae eventually confided in me that her boyfriend was "mean" to her. She denied any physical abuse. She said that listening to and writing about *Breathing Underwater* made her think about her boyfriend and if she really wanted to be with him. She said, "Now I get it. I got plans. I ain't gonna let some guy hold me back. If he ever touch me like that, it'd be over. "

At the end of the whole class focus on *Breathing Underwater*, I did short book talks on books that I had added to the classroom library focused on dating and relationship violence (see Table 1). Unfortunately, I could not find very many books that addressed this issue. I did give Jessica a copy of a short story, "So I Ain't No Good Girl," from *Who Am I Without Him* (Flake, 2004) and asked her to talk with the counselor about it. I know that I am not a counselor or psychologist and that many of our students need this level of support. I also know that when we share readings with our students that help them understand their experiences, they are more likely to seek and accept the help they need.

Suicide

More than 500,000 youth attempt suicide and 5000 youth commit suicide each year (www.teen-depression.info). Every 2 hours and 15 minutes, a person under the age of 25 completes suicide. Given the fact that suicide is the second leading causes of death for young adults ages 15-19, it's hard to imagine a teacher who has not been touched by this epidemic. Teenage suicide is often a result of bullying, intolerance of racial, ethnic or sexual orientation. As noted in the first chapter (Darvin, 2008) students often feel powerless when confronting these social issues in and out of the classroom and without guidance or acknowledgment from a significant adult, they may resort to harmful behaviors rather than seeking help and understanding. Although suicide itself may not be classified as social justice issue, it and violence towards others, has often been cited as resulting from years of social injustices being perpetrated upon the suicide victim.

For more information about the signs of potential suicide in teens see www.suicidology.org.

What can teachers do about this epidemic? Fisher (2005) noted that teachers can have an impact in this area. More specifically, he recommended that teachers have books available in which suicide is dealt with in sensitive ways (see Table 2 for a sample list). These books allow students to understand that they are not the only ones and that they can talk with adults about their feelings. As one of the students recently said to me, "Every student at our school has thought about it [suicide] at least once."

In some schools, the issue of suicide is addressed directly. For example, during the opening weeks of the school year at an urban high school, the silent sustained reading period, which occurs for 20-minutes each day, was suspended. During this time, every teacher read aloud the book *Whirligig* (Fleischman, 1998). A total of 2,300 students heard and discussed this book with their teachers. In the first chapter, Brent goes to party, is rejected, gets drunk, and attempts suicide by closing his eyes and taking his hands off the steering wheel. Of course this meant that the school had to be ready for students to discuss drinking, drinking and driving, and suicide. In many places, this would be forbidden. The faculty at this school wanted their students to know that these were real issues and that every student had a support system.

Teaching Ideas:

- ❖ Suicide prevention centers have a wealth of information about how to help children who may be thinking about suicide. Look at save.org for more information.
- ❖ Bring in the family or friend of someone who has committed suicide to talk about what it has done in their life.
- ❖ Examine the aftermath of suicide and how family members are affected: Anna Nicole Smith, Kurt Cobain, etc.

As one example of the outcome from this schoolwide activity, Marco wrote a letter to one of his teachers and left it on the desk. It said, in part, "I know Brent is white and goes to a private school, but I'm like him." This was Marco's plea for help and his teacher knew it. She arranged for a suicide watch and got Marco into counseling. Clearly Marco had learned that certain topics were "off-limits" in school and could not receive the help he needed until his teacher shared the book with the class.

Fisher (2005) also recommended that teachers regularly monitor students' writing for the suicide warning signs identified above and that professionals be invited into classrooms to discuss suicide with students. Together with books that help students understand that they are not alone, that they are valued and cared about, these efforts can reduce the number of students who take their lives every year.

Sexual Orientation

Being gay, lesbian, bisexual, or transgender and/or adjusting to feelings of attraction to members of the same sex may also present an increased suicide risk (Lock & Steiner, 1999; Garofalo, Wolf, Wissow, Woods, Goodman, 1999). This was portrayed in the Showtime series *Huff*, in which the opening episode graphically displays a gay teenager's suicide while in his psychiatrist's office.

More importantly, our adolescent students who are struggling with their sexual orientation can use literature to understand their thoughts, feelings, and experiences. Having said that, this topic is taboo in many communities. Dating violence and suicide are difficult enough to discuss in school, and may in fact be forbidden topics. Discussing homosexuality in schools raises even more red flags for administrators and community members. In many places, teachers cannot read "sensitive topics" books aloud with the whole class unless the parents give consent. In many of these same places, however, it is acceptable to have books on the bookshelves for students to read on their own.

Teaching Ideas:

❖ Have students count how many times during hallway passing they hear the word gay or faggot in the 10 minutes it takes to get to the next class. What other insults do they hear? Explore these words and why homosexuality is so scary for them.

❖ Have students take action. Start an after school club for Gay/Lesbian students.

❖ Talk about gay and lesbian issues in the classroom. You may have gay and lesbian students and students with two mommies or two daddies – school is the place to talk about discomfort with homosexuality and their understandings of homosexuality.

❖ Watch the movie, "It's Elementary: Talking about Gay Issues in the Classroom" to learn how different teachers address homosexuality in their schools. This movie shows classrooms ranging from kindergarten through high school talking about gay issues in the classroom.

This is not to say that it isn't important to help adolescents learn about themselves. Until Tonja read *Empress of the World* (Ryan, 2002), she thought that she was the only girl who liked other girls. Similarly, until Max read *Geography Club* (Hartinger, 2003) and *Boy Meets Boy* (Levithan, 2003), he was a passive, unengaged student. He says that reading these books made him realize, "I'm normal and I want a club like everyone else." He started a Gay-Straight Alliance and a lunch-time bookclub. It was interesting to observe a number of students, straight and gay, discuss *Alt Ed* (Atkins, 2003) and debate whether or not the counselor was right and if people who were really so different could get along.

One of the most touching reactions Max made came after he read the second volume of *Sevens* (Wallens, 2002) in which the whole school finds out that Jeremy is gay. Max wrote a poem about his new understanding that he could have a meaningful relationship with another person, and the world, even though he was gay.

> Alone
> Leper, hated, feared
> Doomed to sit on the side of life
> Never to be touched, never to be loved
> Unless
> My friends still care
> Unless
> My family loves me
> Unless
> Teachers respect me
> Can I, dare I, wish
> I'm still me
> Looking for my Jeremy
> I'm still me

Conclusions

Reading does many things for the mind. We read to find out things and we read to learn how to do things. We also read for pleasure and enjoyment. Literature provides us with opportunities to meet people we might never get to meet and to visit places we may never see. And importantly especially for adolescents, literature provides an opportunity to learn about oneself – an opportunity that rarely presents itself in other ways.

While there are endless things that adolescents need to learn about themselves, we have focused on three topics that are rarely addressed in secondary schools today. These topics are closely related to the social justice foundation on which this book was developed. If students do not feel comfortable with themselves, up to an including the point at which they attempt or commit suicide, we have not done our jobs. Quality literature can open doors and provide students with access to the supports, resources, and development they need.

Research Projects

1. Interview four to six adolescents. Ask them about the "big issues" in their lives. What do they want to think about that could be address through literature?
2. Select a target book and create standards-aligned lessons around it. It's not enough to simply read a book aloud, the book should also provide an opportunity for students to develop their reading comprehension and/or literary analysis skills.

Making a Difference

1. Start a club – lunch or afterschool – in which students can read literature that allows them to consider their lives from another perspective. This could be a group of male students who have a history of violence, students who have been victims of relationship violence, students who are questioning their gender or sexual orientation, or students who have been victims of hate crimes.
2. Create a classroom library that is inclusive of the issues addressed in this chapter. Regularly conduct book talks in which you "sanction" books that students can read independently and discuss with you.
3. Identify students at risk of violence or suicide and make a pact with them. Help them access supports and services at school and maintain a relationship with them that shows you care.

Other Resources

Table 1: Books that address dating and relationship violence

Clarke, K. A. (2004). *The breakable vow.* New York: Harper Collins.

Dessen, S. (2000). *Dreamland.* New York: Puffin.

Flinn, A. (2001). *Breathing underwater.* New York: HarperTempest.

Miklowitz, G. (1995). *Past forgiving.* New York: Simon & Schuster.

Tashjian, J. (2003). *Faultline.* New York: Henry Hold and Company.

Table 2: Books that address suicide

Fields, T. (2002). *After the death of Anna Gonzales.* New York: Henry Holt & Company.

Fleischman, P. (1998). *Whirligig.* New York: Dell Laurel-Leaf.

Frank, E. R. (2000). *Life is funny.* New York: Dorling Kindersley Publishing.

Frank, E. R. (2002). *America.* New York: Simon Pulse.

Mickle, S. F. (2001). *The turning hour.* Montgomery, AL: River City.

Myers, W. D. (2004). *Shooter.* New York: HarperTempest.

Picoult, J. (1999). *The pact: A love story.* New York: Perennial.

Runyon, B. (2004). *The burn journals.* New York: Alfred A. Knopf.

Sparks, B. (Ed.). (1979). *Jay's journal.* New York: Pocket Books.

Trueman, T. (2003). *Inside out.* New York: HarperTempest.

Vaught, S. (2006). *Trigger.* New York: Bloomsbury.

Wittlinger, E. (2001). *Razzle.* New York: Simon Pulse.

Table 3: Gay-, Lesbian-, Bisexual-, and Transgender-affirming books

Atkins, C. (2003). *Alt ed.* New York: G. P. Putnam's Sons.

Bauer, M. D. (1995). *Am I blue?* New York: HarperTrophy.

Hartinger, B. (2003). *Geography club.* New York: HarperTempest.

Heron, A. (1995). *Two teenagers in twenty: Writings by gay and lesbian youth.* New York: Alyson.

Howe, J. (2005). *Totally Joe.* New York: Atheneum Books for Young Readers.

Kerr, M. E. (1995). *Deliver us from Evie.* New York: HarperTrophy.

Larochelle, D. (2005). *Absolutely, positively not...* New York: Arthur Levine.

Levithan, D. (2003). *Boy meets boy.* New York: Knopf.

Peters, J. A. (2003). *Keeping you a secret.* New York: Little, Brown, & Company.

Peters, J. A. (2004). *Luna.* New York: Little, Brown, & Company.

Peters, J. A. (2005). *Far from Xanadu.* New York: Little, Brown, & Company.

Peters, J. A. (2006). *Between mom and Jo.* New York: Little, Brown, & Company.

Ryan, S. (2002). *Empress of the world.* New York: Penguin.

Sanchez, A. (2001). *Rainbow high.* New York: Simon & Schuster.

Sanchez, A. (2003). *Rainbow boys.* New York: Simon & Schuster.

Sanchez, A. (2005). *Rainbow road.* New York: Simon & Schuster.

Sanchez, A. (2003). *So hard to say.* New York: Simon & Schuster.

Wallens, S. (2002). *Sevens.* New York: Puffin.

Wittlinger, E. (2001). *Hard love.* New York: Simon Pulse.

Wittlinger, E. (2001). *Razzle.* New York: Simon Pulse.

References

Bishop, R. S. (1994). *Kaleidoscope: A multicultural booklist for grades K-8.* Urbana, IL: National Council of Teachers of English.

Garofalo, R., Wolf, C., Wissow, L. S., Woods, E. R., Goodman, E. (1999). Sexual orientation and risk of suicide attempts among a representative sample of youth. *Archives of Pediatrics and Adolescent Medicine,* 153, 487-493.

Fisher, D. (2004). Setting the "opportunity to read" standard: Resuscitating the SSR program in an urban high school. *Journal of Adolescent & Adult Literacy,* 48, 138-151.

Fisher, D. (2005). The literacy educator's role in suicide prevention. *Journal of Adolescent & Adult Literacy,* 48, 364-373.

Fisher, D., Obidah, J. E., Pelton, M. H., & Campana, J. (2005). Violence as a factor in the lives of urban youth. In J. Flood & P. Anders (Eds.), *Literacy development of students in urban schools: Research and policy* (pp. 68-96). Newark, DE: International Reading Association.

Flake, S. (2004). *Who am I without him? Short stories about girls and the boys in their lives.* New York: Jump at the Sun/Hyperion Books for Children.

Flowers, R. B. (2002). *Kids who commit adult crimes: Serious criminality by juvenile offenders.* Binghamton, NY: Haworth Press.

Funk, R.E., & Berkowitz, A. D. (2000). *Preventing sexual violence: A simple matter of justice.* Paper presented at the National Sexual Violence Prevention Conference, Dallas, TX.

Howard, D. E., & Wang, M. Q. (2003). Risk profiles of adolescent girls who were victims of dating violence. *Adolescence,* 38(149), 1-14.

Lock, J., & Steiner, H. (1999). Gay, lesbian, and bisexual youths' risks for emotional, physical, and social problems: Results from a community-based survey. *Journal of Child and Adolescent Psychiatry*, 1, 297-304.

Moss, B., & Hendershot, J. (2002) Exploring sixth graders' selection of nonfiction trade books. *The Reading Teacher*, 56, 6-17.

Richardson, J. S., & Boyle, J. (1998). A read-aloud for discussing disabilities. *Journal of Adolescent & Adult Literacy*, 41, 684-686.

Sleeter, C. E. (1996). *Multicultural education as social activism*. Albany: State University of New York Press.

Chapter 4

Social Activism through Books about Child Labor

Linda Lamme

Consider:

Naturally, looking at child labor involves us in thinking about many issues about social justice.

❖ *How would a teacher talk about this?*

❖ *Is this a justifiable use of curricular time?*

❖ *What children's literature is available examining children in the workforce?*

Children are naturally interested in the lives of other children; therefore, child labor makes an excellent vehicle for promoting a social justice curriculum in upper elementary and middle school classrooms. Award-winning books about child labor can frame units of study and culminate in social action channeled through anti-child labor groups. Children throughout history labored with the rest of their families, on farms and in other workplaces. In this country many children also labored outside the home to provide money for their family's survival. By reading award-winning books, students can learn much about American history and about the role of children in this nation's development. These books include stories about children who took action to end child labor and the harsh practices that accompanied it. Using the information and the experiences of children in historical books as a model, students can then read about child labor that exists today and become activists to help halt these practices.

Child Labor in America

The Smithsonian Institution National Museum of American History online provides an excellent introduction to child labor (Sweatshops in America). A class can take a virtual field trip to learn about child labor in this country from 1820 – 1997. The Child Labor Public Education Project provides an overview of child labor worldwide and historically in the United States (Child Labor Project). By 1890, 19% of children between the ages of 10 and 15 years were employed in factories. (History Matters).

Several nonfiction informational books cover a wide spectrum of child labor, such as *Kids at Work: Lewis Hine and the Crusade against Child Labor* (Freedman, 1994), a book based on the photographs taken by Lewis Hine who was employed as an investigative reporter for the National Child Labor Committee in the early 20th Century. A teacher might share this book by reading parts of it orally to the entire class and leaving the book in a place where students can use it as a resource. Hine's photos were instrumental in obtaining child labor laws in this country. A number of Lewis Hine's pictures are available at "The History Place" website.

Phillip Hoose's *It's Our World, Too!* (1993), and *We Were Here, Too!* (2001), are collected biographies of young people in American history that include farm workers, newsies, sweatshop workers, and civil rights workers. Read aloud a few of the biographies and leave the books in the classroom for students to peruse on their own. After an initial introduction to this topic, viewing the websites and reading aloud from informational books and biographies, it is time to group students for reading projects, but it is still a good idea to continue reading aloud from the nonfiction books throughout the unit.

Books about Child Labor in America

Depending upon how many books are available through your school and public library, combine related books into sets and obtain multiple copies of books so that there are enough books for each student to read. The books feature boy and girl main characters and multiple ethnicities and races. The nonfiction informational books provide a complete history of child labor and the labor movement, while the novels provide personal stories about child laborers. The nonfiction books contain actual photos, many by Lewis Hine, an investigative reporter who took photos of child laborers in mills, in mines, and on the streets. The nonfiction books also contain extensive bibliographies that can be used for further investigation. Combining the two sources, fiction and nonfiction, students can learn details as well as an overview of American history in this era.

Children's Books about Child Laborers in the United States

Book Title	Author	Location	Genre
Slave workers			
Silent Thunder	Pinkney	Virginia	HF Novel
Miles' Song	McGill	South Carolina	HF Novel
Civil War Soldiers			
When Johnny Went Marching	Wisler	Many places	Nonfiction
No Man's Land	Bartoletti	Georgia	HF Novel
Soldier's Heart	Paulsen	Pennsylvania	HF Novel
Pink and Say	Polacco	Georgia	HF Pic Bk
Lil Dan, The Drummer Boy	Bearden	The South	HF Pic Bk
Farm Laborers (Historical)			
Up Before Daybreak	Hopkinson	The South	Nonfiction
Song of Sampo Lake	Durbin	Minnesota	HF Novel
Jake's Orphan	Brooke	North Dakota	HF Novel
Worth	LaFaye	Nebraska	HF Novel
Gib Rides Home	Snyder	Midwest	HF Novel
Bkackwater Ben	Durbin	Minnesota	HF Novel
Migrant Workers			
Esperanza Rising	Ryan	California	HF Novel
The Circuit	Jimenez	Many places	Memoirs
Breaking Through	Jimenes	Many places	Memoirs
Under the Same Sky	DeFelice	Upstate New York	HF Novel
Mill Workers			
Mother Jones and the Mill Children	Coleman	Pennsylvania	Nonfiction
Kids on Strike	Bartoletti	Northeast	Nonfiction
Hear My Sorrow	Hopkinson	New York City	Diary
Lyddie	Paterson	Lowell, MA	HF Novel
Ashes of Roses	Auch	New York City	HF Novel
Miners			
Growing Up in Coal Country	Bartoletti	Pennsylvania	Nonfiction
The Breaker Boys	Hughes	Pennsylvania	HF Novel
The Journal of Otto Peltonen	Durbin	Minnesota	HF Novel
Railroad Workers			
Coolies	Yin	West	HF Pic Bk
The Journal of Sean Sullivan	Durbin	West	HF Novel
True Heart	Moss	West	HF Pic Bk
Street Vendors and Newsies			
Joshua's Song	Harlow	Boston	HF Novel
Kid Blink Beats the World	Brown	New York City	HF Novel
The King of Mulberry Street	Napoli	New York City	HF Novel

Study groups will enjoy the books and learn American history in the process. Because these books have won numerous children's book awards, they should be readily available at school and public libraries. It is important to use award-winning books because there they are accurate and well written unlike many of the series books, which are poorly written and contain oversimplified and inaccurate information. A good source of well-written books on social studies topics in general is the annual NCSS Notable Book Award List at (www.socialstudies.org/resources/notable/).

Child Labor Outside the United States

After the historical unit is completed, provide a transition into the study of child labor today. The historical books on child labor in America set the stage for activism by providing examples of child labor and in the case of newsies and mill workers, telling the stories of child activists who went on strike for better wages and working conditions. To transition into the books on global child labor, link these historical types of child labor in our country to information about the same kinds of labor today worldwide. Today there are laws in many countries that limit the amount of legal child labor, but children still are forced to work just about everywhere in the world.

After students have read and discussed books, it is helpful to provide them with websites to update their information and see how similar types of child labor exist today in other parts of the world. Although the U.N. Supplementary Convention on the Abolition of Slavery abolished slavery (and bonded labor) in 1956, millions of children still work in bonded labor (Human Rights Watch). According to the Human Rights Watch, children are direct participants in war in over twenty countries around the world. An estimated 200,000 to 300,000 children are serving as soldiers for both rebel groups and government forces in current armed conflicts. Of nearly 250 million children involved in child labor, however, the majority, over 70 percent, work in agriculture.

Teaching Idea:

❖ While students are reading their books, have them search the Internet and the school library media center for more information about their form of child labor. Each group then can present a report to classmates on their child labor topic and the books, and groups can be reformed for further reading and study.

The International Labor Association claims that in 2006, 250 million children between the ages of five and fourteen worked in developing countries. Sixty-one percent of these are in Asia, 32 percent in Africa, and 7 percent in Latin America (Promises Broken). In the United States, the plight of migrant workers has been well documented and can be compared to child labor problems in developing countries. Children in child labor experience more disease, mental health problems and earlier death than non-working children, and the problem is getting worse each year.

Statistics from the Human Rights Watch are amazing. Children as young as six routinely work in sugar cane fields in El Salvador. Over 600,000 children ages 8 and higher, work on banana plantations and packing plants in Equador. Even in the United States, over 300,000 children ages 12 and higher work in large-scale commercial agriculture. There are 15 million bonded child laborers in India, most of whom are Salits (untouchables) and well over half of these are children who work in agriculture, tending crops, herding cattle, and performing other tasks for their masters. Many work in the silk industry boiling cocoons, removing worms, and reeling and twisting the threads. Over a million children a year between the ages of 7 and 12, manually remove pests from cotton plants in Egypt (Human Rights Watch Backgrounder). In the Kathmandu valley in Nepal, 50,000 people work as weavers and another 100,000 do carding, spinning, drying, washing, and transport. Of these, 1800 are children under the age of 14. Carpets are Nepal's number 1 export, bringing in $135 million a year (Charle, 2001).

A good place to start a study of child labor outside the United States is to obtain a map of Asia and plot the locations of child labor novels. Students will see that the novels are set in China and Thailand, and in the rug making industries of India and Pakistan. Since there are only four novels, provide multiple copies of each so that four groups of students can read the books as a literature circle and then meet to discuss the stories. If you cannot obtain multiple copies, create a nonfiction group and rotate the books. To focus on aesthetic responses (Rosenblatt, 1995) students might discuss how they felt as they read the stories. The responses might include feelings such as sadness, misery, or depression or anger, irritation, annoyance, or even rage or fury. Then use the same guidelines as with historical fiction to analyze the child labor in the books. At this point the stage is set for the groups to explore the nonfiction books to learn the facts about child labor worldwide, and to plan strategies for taking action to help reduce child labor.

Book Title	Author	Location	Genre
Historical Fiction Books about International Child Labor			
Spilled Water	Grindley	China	Servant; Toy factory
Chu Ju's House	Whelan	China	Gutting fish; silk factory
Silk Umbrellas	Marsden	Thailand	Radio factory; painting umbrellas
Iqbal	D'Adamo	Pakistan	Carpet factory

Nonfiction Books About International Child Labor

Child labor occurs around the world. Fortunately, nonfiction books contain resources that will be useful in planning an activist reader response curriculum. When students read the informational books, they can make a list of opportunities for action to combat child labor. Then, go to the Internet to determine which organizations the class might like to contact to determine how they might join this worldwide effort to eradicate child labor.

Listen to Us: The World's Working Children (Springer, 1997) is a photo essay that pictures child laborers, including migrant workers, brick-makers, garbage pickers, and bonded laborers, whose stories are heartbreaking. Jane Springer has worked overseas for ten years with organizations such as UNESCO and has witnessed the labor about which she writes. There are many sidebars, maps, and charts in this exhaustive treatment of the topic. This book contains an index, glossary, and bibliography, making it a wonderful resource for the study of child labor and an excellent book to review the conventions of nonfiction informational books.

Several books focus on the rug mills in India and Pakistan where hundreds of thousands of children at young ages tie knots to create rugs. Susan Kuklin's nonfiction title, *Iqbal Masih and the Crusaders Against Child Slavery* (1998) chronicles the life of Iqbal Masih, a Pakistani rug weaver, who was sold into slavery at the age of four and freed by a human rights group at 10, when he became a crusader against child slavery in Pakistan, Europe, and the United States. He returned home to Pakistan at age 12, where he was murdered. His death alerted the world to the horrible working conditions of children enslaved at young ages. Iqbal's work inspired other authors to write about child bondage and become instrumental in establishing child labor laws. Of especial importance to teachers, is the last section of the book that describes what human rights groups are doing to organize protests and boycotts of goods made with child labor.

Teaching Idea:

❖ Do a short book talk about each book and have students select books. Form groups by type of child labor in the books selected, depending upon how many books are available on these topics. Search for books across the libraries in your school district and to supplement those with books from the local public library. Let family members know in advance about this assignment so that they can talk to their children about their own family history in case the students want to explore a type of labor that was in their family background.

Another nonfiction book, *Stolen Dreams: Portraits of Working Children* (Parker, Engfer and Conrow, 1998), contains a chapter about Iqbal, but also pictorial and written documentation of working children in Nepal, India, Bangladesh, and Mexico. Parker, an occupational health physician in Minnesota, has traveled to investigate children at work as farm workers, carpet weavers, brick makers, and soldiers. The non-exploitive photos in this book tell the story of child labor in many places around the world. The information provides examples of actions taken by school children including letters and speeches by American kids, who call for boycotts and other action. The book also provides a detailed bibliography, a list of resources, and organizations to contact.

Children will be fascinated by the voices of former child workers in biographical literature. *Jhalak Man Tamang: slave labor whistle-blower* (Miller, 2007) shares the story of Jhalak, a ten-year old who was sold to a carpet master in Katmandu to work daily from 4AM to 11PM knotting woolen rugs on heavy wooden looms. Like Iqbal, he is rescued and shares his story in an effort to end child labor. In We Need to go to School: Voices of the Rugmark Children (Roberts-Davis, 2001), twenty former child carpet weavers in Nepal describe their working conditions as child slaves and send out a call to the world to save the children still laboring in the factories. The author, Tanya Roberts-Davis, was only 16 when she visited the Rugmark centers in 1999. Fortunately the book provides information on organizations where students could become active. Students could each read a different story, then share the child's experiences orally, perhaps taking the role of the child. Such brief talks could make a short assembly program, turning this project into a school-wide campaign. Or, the teacher could read aloud several of the stories.

Activism Projects

According to the Rugmark website, one in six children in the world today works illegally and nearly 300,000 are exploited in the carpet industry to weave carpets for American and European markets. Funded by a number of philanthropy groups, Rugmark has been working on reducing the number of child laborers in India, Nepal, and Pakistan by setting up schools near rug factories and conducting inspections of the factories to be sure children are not laborers. In the United States, Rugmark labels rugs that are not created with child labor and makes efforts to educate people to purchase those rugs instead of the many others without labels.

Teaching Idea:

❖ Students can canvas stores in their communities to find out which carry rugs with the Rugmark brand. They can publicize which stores do or do not sell these rugs and ask storeowners to find out about Rugmark products. Letters to the editor or even informational articles on Rugmark and child labor for a local newspaper can create community support for a boycott of stores that sell rugs created by child laborers

Child labor laws in the United States are not being enforced as well as they were in the 1980's and the penalties for infractions are far less than allowed by law (Child Labor Coalition). This information, too, can be publicized as a way to support children who are forced to work. Students might also raise money to send to nonprofit organizations that act to stop child labor, such as The Global Fund for Children. On this website there are suggestions for how children can support their grant funds that are given to projects to help children worldwide.

In the long run, however, it is important to support organizations like Rugmark that actually place child laborers in school, as the only permanent solution to child labor is education and the possibility for family incomes to increase. If poverty is the ultimate cause of child labor, only a redistribution of wealth will solve the problem, (Child Labor Project). That may be beyond the realm of children in today's classrooms.

Children's Books Cited

Auch, M. (2002). *Ashes of roses.* New York: Henry Holt.

Bartoletti, S. (1996). *Growing up in coal country.* Boston: Houghton Mifflin.

Bartoletti, S. C. (1999). *Kids on Strike!* Boston: Houghton Mifflin.

Bartoletti, S .C. (1999). *No man's land: A young soldier's story.* New York: Blue Sky.

Bearden, R. (2003). *Li'l Dan, the drummer boy: a Civil War story,* New York: Simon & Schuster.

Brooke, Debbie. (2000). *Jake's orphan.* New York: DK.

Brown, D, (2004). *Kid Blink beats the world.* Millbrook/Roaring Brook.

Coleman, P. (1994). *Mother Jones and the Mill Children.* Brookfield, CT: Millbrook.

D'Adamo, F. (2003). *Iqbal.* Translated by An Leonori. New York: Atheneum.

DeFelice, C. (2003). *Under the same sky.* New York: Farrar, Straus and Giroux.

Durbin, W. (2003). *Blackwater Ben.* New York: Wendy Lamb.

Durbin, W. (2000). *The journal of Otto Peltonen, a Finnish immigrant.* New York: Scholastic.

Durbin, W. (1999). *The journal of Sean Sullivan: A transcontinental railroad worker.* New York: Scholastic.

Durbin, W. (2002). *Song of Sampo Lake.* New York: Wendy Lamb.

Freedman, R. (1994). *Kids at Work: Lewis Hine and the crusade against child labor.* Photographs by Lewis Hine. New York: Clarion.

Grindley, S. (2004). *Spilled Water.* New York: Bloomsbury.

Harlow, J. H. (2002). *Joshua's song*. New York: Margaret K. McElderry.

Hoose, P. (1993). *It's our world, too!* Boston: Little Brown.

Hoose, P. (2001). *We were here, too!* New York: Farrar, Straus and Giroux.

Hopkinson, D. (2004). *Hear my sorrow: the diary of Angela Denoto, a shirtwaist worker.* New York: Scholastic.

Hopkinson, D. (2006). *Up before daybreak: Cotton and people in America.* New York: Scholastic.

Hughes, P. (2004). *The breaker boys.* New York: Farrar Straus and Giroux.

Jimenez, F. (2001). *Breaking through.* Boston, Houghton Mifflin.

Jimenez, F. (1999). *The circuit: Stories from the life of a migrant child.* Boston: Houghton Mifflin.

Kuklin, S. (1998). *Iqbal Masih and the crusaders against child slavery.* New York: Henry Holt.

LaFaye, A. (2004). *Worth.* New York: Simon and Schuster.

Marsden, C. (2004). *Silk umbrellas.* Cambridge, MA: Candlewick.

McGill, A. (2000). *Mile's song.* Boston: Houghton Mifflin.

Miller, R. H. (2007). *Jhalak Man Tamang: slave labor whistleblower.* Detroit: KidHaven Press.

Moss, M. (1999). *True heart.* San Diego: Silver Whistle.

Napoli, D. J. (2005). *The king of Mulberry Street.* New York: Wendy Lamb.

Parker, D. L., Engfer, L, and Conrow, R. (1998). *Stolen dreams: portraits of working children.* Photographs by David L. Parker. Minneapolis: Lerner.

Paterson, K. (1991). *Lyddie.* New York: Lodestar.

Paulsen, G. (1998). *Soldier's heart: A novel of the Civil War.* New York: Delacorte.

Polacco, P. (1994). *Pink and Say.* New York: Philomel.

Pinkney, A. D. (1999). *Silent Thunder.* Hyperion.

Roberts-Davis. (2001). *We need to go to school: Voices of the Rug-mark children*. Toronto: Douglas McIntyre.

Ryan, P. M. (2000). *Esperanza rising*. Scholastic.

Springer, J. Listen to us: *The world's working children*. Toronto: Douglas McIntire

Snyder, S. K. (1998). *Gib Rides Home*. New York: Delacorte.

Wisler, G. C. (2001). *When Johnny went marching: Young Americans fight the Civil War*. New York: Harper Collins.

Yin. (2001). *Coolies*. Illus. Chris Soentpiet. New York: Philomel.

Whelan, G. (2004). *Chu Ju's house*. New York: HarperCollins.

Other Suggested Projects

Setting Survey

Post a map of the United States on a wall so that each student can plot the location of their story by placing a number on the map at the location of their book, and writing the number and title of the book on a piece of notebook paper as a key posted next to the map. Likewise, students can write the name of their book on a timeline stretched along a wall of the classroom. At the end of the presentations it will become clear that child labor existed all over this nation at different times in our history. Students who are avid readers may want to read more than one book about their form of child labor and students will enjoy reading books that other groups recommend as well. If time permits, stay on one set of books for a week, then rotate. Depending on how much time the students have for reading, they might be able to read a book a week and participate in three different groups based on stories about three different types of child labor

Group Literature Discussions

Establish a home reading program where students take their books home nightly and read for half an hour. Provide for half an hour of sustained silent reading from the books each day in the classroom.

Using this schedule, students should be able to read a book a week. In class have students meet several times a week with their child labor group to discuss the books they are reading. A guide sheet for recording information from the fiction books might contain the following questions:

- How old was the main character?
- What did the character do for labor?
- What were the challenges and what were the benefits of their labor?
- Why did children need to perform this kind of work?
- How did the labor impact the young person's life (ie schooling, future employment and health)?
- What eventually stopped children from performing this kind of labor?

I Search

As a supplement to the unit, have students ask elder family members and any elders they know if any of their ancestors were child laborers. Since all but American Indians were immigrants to this land at some point in time, it is likely that some students have ancestors who were, in fact, child laborers. Students can write their family stories about the child labor of their ancestors or family friends or about child labor that existed at the location of their school. Some students might not be able to find out this information, so it should be a voluntary supplement to the curriculum. A local history museum might also contain information about child labor in the region of the school or in the nation and might provide a valuable field trip. Older citizens in the community who had family members who experienced child labor make guest speakers for this unit.

Research and Teach

Students can study where the clothing they wear is made and by whom. They can then look the companies up on the Internet and at the Human Rights Watch to see if they use child labor. Then they can educate their schoolmates and the community through posters, information on a website, and booths at town fairs, to inform others about their discoveries. Eventually a whole town or city might boycott items created by child labor and press to get local business establishments to market only items made by adults.

References

Charle, S, (2001). Nepal: Children of the looms. *The Globalist*. Accessed December 27, 2006). http://www.theglobalist.com/DBWeb/StoryId.aspx?StoryId=2092

Child Labor Coalition: http://www.stopchildlabor.org/

Child Labor Project: http://www.continuetolearn.uiowa.edu/laborctr/child_labor/

Global Fund for Children: http://www.globalfundforchildren.org

History Matters: http://historymatters.gmu.edu/d/6967

History Place: http://www.historyplace.com/unitedstates/childlabor/.

History Place: Child Labor in America, 1908-1912. Photos by Lewis W. Hine: http://www.historyplace.com/unitedstates/childlabor/

Human Rights Watch: http://www.hrw.org/children/child-legal.htm

Human Rights Watch Backgrounder: http://hrw.org/backgrounder/crp/back0610.htm

Promises Broken: http://www.hrw.org/campaigns/crp/promises/labor.html.

Rosenblatt, L. (1995). *Literature as exploration*. New York: Modern Language Association of America.

RUGMARK Foundation: www.rugmark.org

Sweatshops in America: Smithsonian Institution National Museum of American History and Office of Exhibits Central: http://americanhistory.si.edu/sweatshops/intro/intro.htm

Chapter 5

Using Children's Literature to Teach for Social Justice:

Critical Literacy and Language Rights

Bobbie Kabuto

Consider:

❖ *How can a critical literacy perspective be fostered with very young children?*

❖ *Why is it important to expose young children to multiple languages in the classroom?*

❖ *What does it mean to be bilingual? What does it mean to be bi-literate?*

Teaching for social justice and democratic classrooms takes everyday classroom routines and changes them into transformative experiences in which children become critical and collaborative agents in their learning and the learning of others. Taking this stance means moving away from preordained curriculum to make it jointly created, interpreted, and negotiated with the students. Teaching for social justice is not an outlined model, but a way that we frame and imagine our teaching (Taylor, 2005). Although this can be difficult for many of us, it can be particularly difficult with young children because we have it ingrained in us that we wear a particular type of "teacher hat" that privileges culturally acceptable ways to teach reading through activities such as the alphabet, onset and rhyme, word clusters, picture clues, and reading strategies. However, learning to read also means learning to read the world (Freire, 2003). In order to do so, children must see how reading allows them voices, multiple social and cultural identities and helps them to understand the world around them in ways that positively impact their lives. This becomes the motivating factor for children to seek out and reread books that in turn teach them the skills of reading (Meek, 1988). In this manner, books become safe spaces of inquiry to explore and challenge real life issues while shaping and challenging who they are in this world (Wolk, 2004).

Teachers can take an inquiry stance through critical literacy in early childhood classrooms to address the linguistic diversity of writers and, in turn, the children in our classrooms. This stance is premised on a social justice framework around language rights. In other places, I have argued that literacy in multiple languages is the right that all children have for their social, cognitive, linguistic, and emotional development (Kabuto, 2006; Taylor & Kabuto, In press). Children learn to read and write in multiple languages as a way to develop and learn about themselves by creating and maintaining social and cultural relationships and identities with others.

Take for example my five year-old daughter who was learning English and Japanese. When she wrote a birthday card on Valentines Day to her Japanese speaking friend, she wrote "Happy Valentines Day" in English and "From Emma to Erika" in Japanese. The choices that she made were based on the relationships that she wanted to create or maintain: English for an American holiday and Japanese for her Japanese speaking friend. By using both languages together, she developed an identity of not only a writer, but also as a person who interacts within multiple spaces in the world.

Allowing children the right to choose among different modes and means of expression through multiple written languages and sign systems, we can see the complexity that being bi/multiliterate entails. When we privilege one language (English) or one way (written language) over other meaningful ways that children use to create not just linguistic meaning, but also social and cultural meanings related to identity, social structure, rights, and privileges, we reduce the complexity of learning to isolated, codeable parts of language. Language is no longer a right, but a social milieu in which children are socialized into inequalities around language and literacy.

Schools and classrooms can be transformative places that can challenge social, cultural, and linguistic inequalities. Recent political moves place status on English over other languages, promote the banking system of education (Freire, 2003), and privilege inert ideas (Whitehead, 1929) over caring, empathy, compassion, social imagination and equality. Critical literacy in classrooms can recapture the space where creative and productive dialogues can take place around linguistic and language rights.

John Dewey's (1916) work helps to lay a theoretical foundation for conceptualizing critical literacy in early childhood classrooms. Dewey (1916) argued that young children held a particular type of power in their flexibility to form habits of mind and that education could cultivate ways that dissolved barriers of race, class, and gender. A democratic education, from Dewey's standpoint, also has the potential to repudiate linguistic prejudices.

Not just children, but also teachers imagine venues that bring public spaces to the private lives where they can initiate their voices in concepts of freedom, equality, and social justice. A critical literacy perspective in early childhood classrooms means that children learn to read and write to learn, to shape, and to self-renew within multiple symbolic spaces: linguistic, social, cultural, within which they participate.

Picture Books as Open Spaces

Picture books provide the open spaces that link private and public worlds to teach for social justice. Through picture books children can begin dialogues and conversations about the ways in which and why authors use multiple languages. Take for example, Mice and Beans by Pam Munoz Ryan (2001). On the first page, Ryan (2001) writes,

> Rosa Maria lived in a tiny house with a tiny yard. But she had a big heart, a big family, and more than anything, she loved to cook big meals for them. In one week, her youngest grandchild, Little Catalina, would be seven years old, and the whole family would squeeze into her *casita* for the party. Rosa Maria didn't mind because she believe what her mother had always said, "When there's room in the heart, there's room in the house except for a mouse." (italics present, p. 1)

Instead of *house*, Ryan choose *casita* as she did with other words such as dulces ('candy') and *no importa* ('it doesn't matter') This question may provide a pathway to larger political, cultural, and social issues around language choice and who has the right to make those choices.

Ryan's incorporation of multiple languages encourages the exploration between these issues and her personal history and biography that children need to explore in order to find explanations to the questions that they begin to raise. As children engage in these conversations, they relate their own experiences around language and literacy to understand the author's experiences that affected language choice in written text. Children from multilingual families explore the relationships between languages, writing, and power as they relate to language loss, language across generations, and language as a connector to familial ties. Children who come from monolingual homes can explore the language history in their families to find connections from the past to the present for a better future.

On another plane, these types of conversations develop an eye for writing and enhance how children craft stories. Far too often we forget that children have the potential to read like writers who can envision their own possibilities for writing using multiple written languages. As children craft stories with multiple written languages, they craft their identities and build habits of mind that add new dimensions to their voices, the imagination, the world around them, and challenge dominate ways of using language in schools and society.

Critical Literacy in Practice: *The Umbrella*

The work of Vasquez (2004), whose approach to critical literacy in early childhood classroom, has been influential in conceptualizing a critical approach to studying language rights. As I mentioned before, planning and organizing a critical literacy approach to curriculum is a lived and negotiated experience. Thus it is important to allow children to raise and document questions, find explanations and have the critical conversations that evolve out of the classroom experiences. An audit trail, a public display of artifacts, becomes a critical tool in documenting these transformations in the developing curriculum. The idea behind an audit trail is that it tracks the movement of ideas and is visible to all in the classroom and school community (Vasquez, 2004). Artifacts may consists of photographs, book covers, letters, written conversations, diagrams, and shared writings and cover a bulletin board or a blank wall.

There are 5 main components to the study of language rights using an audit trial. I want to preface this discussion with although these are 5 common components that I have found when taking a critical literacy approach, they may be adjusted or added to by teachers and students. Children should have agency in developing ideas and constructing the trail, and teachers should work with a display and procedure that is most comfortable to them.

To illustrate a study of language rights, I will use the book *Umbrella* by Taro Yashima (1958), which provides an excellent example of how an author's personal history, language identities, and social relationships with others influence how he wrote stories. The *Umbrella*, a Caldecott Honor book, is about a little girl Momo who was given rubber boots and an umbrella for her birthday. Momo waits for the day that it will rain so she can use her umbrella. Yashima, a Japanese-American author, uses Chinese characters (or Kanji) to write the following Japanese words: *haru* (spring), *natsu* (summer), *ame* (rain), *momo* (peach), in the top left corner of various pages.

Teaching Idea: How to Choose Books

The success of your inquiry will depend on the quality of the books. Keeping the following factors in mind will assist in selecting high quality literature that will capture children's imagination, interest, and compassion:

❖ Words or phrases in other languages should reflect real, natural language in the native tongue. Teachers should practice how to pronounce the words before reading the book aloud.

❖ Illustrations that incorporate environmental print in other languages are excellent springboards for discussion.

❖ Stories should be well-developed. Books formatted as picture dictionaries will not provide the same affect.

❖ Stories that bring in other issues related to equity, gender, and prejudice should also be encouraged. Sumo Boy by Hirotaka Nakagawa (2006) is about the superhero Sumo Boy. The book is filled with Japanese environmental print while the story lends itself to a critical discussion about gender roles and equity.

❖ Picture books that represent everyday activities as opposed to overgeneralized celebrations are easier for all children to relate to.

❖ Characters in contemporary roles connect to children's lives over characters that existed centuries ago.

❖ Be critical of books that have negative connotations and attitudes about ethnic groups.

❖ Stories set not only in the United States, but also other countries add other dimensions the discussion of language as social, cultural, and political processes.

Beginning the Audit Trail

To begin the audit trail, teachers select and read a picture book (see *How to Choose Books* above) to the class that will engage children in conversations around language. During one such conversation with the *Umbrella*, a second grade student in my class asked me what the Chinese writing said. This prompted me to return to the book to discuss the Chinese characters and so our audit trail began (see Figure 1: The Audit Trail Outline). We spent time discussing the Chinese characters, which allowed me to return to the book to say that Momo's parents lived in Japan and that maybe the words were not Chinese, but instead that maybe Chinese characters could also be used to write in Japanese.

The children became engaged in the conversation talking about how they know some Chinese words or someone who could speak Chinese. I came to the realization that the students took an all-encompassing view of Chinese to incorporate Japanese and Chinese. I suggested to the students that we should investigate Chinese and Japanese further. The reason for this lies in the understanding that children should not only problematize the text, but also their own understandings and knowledge in order to transform and reconstruct their own worlds.

Teaching Idea: Teacher Preparation

❖ The situated negotiation of a critical literacy curriculum does not negate teacher preparation. Teachers need to ensure that they feel comfortable in discussing the issues of language that may arise. Particularly with young children, they may say things without realizing the impact that they might have on other children. Language is a highly sensitive issue because of its strong familial, emotional, and political ties. I recommend that teachers work within their comfort zone and educate themselves about the history of language struggles and rights in the country. Furthermore, teachers ought to be respectful of other languages by researching the language or practicing the pronunciation of unknown words or phrases.

Investigating Language

To encourage children to think about and share their experiences, teachers can ask them to bring in artifacts written in Chinese and Japanese. The artifacts should be shared in class and connected to the audit trail. By examining the artifacts more closely, the children may come to the realization that some of the written languages look different. The teacher's role is important in these types of critical situations. If teachers ignore the students' interests and comments, the audit trail and, hence, the inquiry will end. Teachers should carefully place themselves as mediators to help children synthesize their questions, without giving them the questions themselves. For example, if children start to recognize the differences, ask them what makes them different and what makes them the same? During a similar engagement with my students, they attempted to write what they saw verbalizing how some characters have similar strokes or parts of the characters look like letters in the alphabet.

From this experience, children may want to know more about the differences in written languages which will initiate the class to search out "experts." Teachers and children may ask friends and family members and look in books, magazines, and on the Internet to find defining characteristics that help them to name the different languages on the artifacts that they brought to the audit trail.

Navigating the Audit Trail

The audit trail should move forward. As children become more engaged with the questions around written languages, the audit trail will grow as steps are included and divergences occur. However, it is easy to keep moving forward with questions and forget about their histories. Consequently, teachers should help children navigate the audit trail by showing them the various origins of their inquiry.

In the case of the *Umbrella*, teachers would return back to the first step of the audit trail that raised the issue of Momo's parents coming from Japan and words written in Chinese characters. Through the language investigation in consequent steps of the audit trial, children may have discovered that Japanese consists of three orthographies: hiragana, katakana, and Chinese kanji. Therefore it would make sense why Yashima would write in Japanese with Chinese characters. Yet, in my experiences, this was not the end of the audit trail because one child wanted to know why the author wanted to use another language. When collecting artifacts in other languages, one child brought in a menu written in Chinese and English from a Chinese restaurant, which initiated a conversation about why the menu would be written in both languages to which another child explained that a customer who can only read and write in Chinese may want to eat there. These types of dialogues carried over to the author's intent in the Umbrella, and the curiosity is well noted since the underlying question focuses on the issue of why would Yashima incorporate a language that is not always recognizable by the perceived audience.

Author Studies

Teachers and children cannot delve into this issue without investigating the personal and professional history of the author. Paley's (1997) book *The Girl with the Brown Crayon* shows the power of author studies in encouraging children to connect public and private spheres. Allowing children to reinvent, transact, and view themselves through books and authors' lives provide spaces, where a deeper meaning related to their personal lives, is created.

Taro Yashima is a pseudonym for Jun Atsushi Iwamatsu, who was born in 1908 and died in 1994. Yashima studied art in Tokyo and was jailed when opposing the Japanese military before World War II. In 1939, Yashima and his wife left for the United States to study art, leaving their son Mako behind. Yashima joined the US army and was an artist for the government at which time he chose to work under the name Taro Yashima out of fear of the Japanese government discovering his activities. After the war, Yashima and his wife became permanent residents and returned to Japan for Mako and later Momo was born (Gale, n.d.).

The evaluation of Yashima personal life entangled through political connotations lives through his books and is represented through language. Although I can only conjecture, Yashima lived as a Japanese-American, who had connections to Japan. Some connections were as strong and visible as his son remaining in Japan while he tried to make a life for himself here. His books present this Japanese-American perspective as clearly mirrored in the *Umbrella* whose main character is Momo, Yashima's own daughter. Thus, language adds to the critical bridge that maintains his identity as a Japanese-American writer. Research documents that Yashima's experiences are parallel to many of the children in our classroom to this day (Fu, 2003; Valdes, 1996). The possibility arises for children to work out these types of experiences through the mask of Yashima's stories and history to better understand their own lives.

Some Language Questions Related to Taro Yashima

- Why did he write in Japanese and English?
- How does his life connect to the content of the books?
- Why would he change his name?
- Why did he use a Japanese pseudonym over an English one?
- What if he only wrote the story in English? Would he appear like a different writer? Would the story have had the same meaning?

Picture Books by Taro Yashima

Yashima, T. (1958, 1986). *Umbrella*. New York: Puffin Books.

---. (1966). *The Village Tree*. New York: Viking Press.

---. (1966). *Youngest One*. New York: Viking Press.

---. (1967). *Seashore Story*. New York: Viking Press.

---. (1976). *Crow Boy*. New York: Puffin Books.

Yashima, M. & Yashima, T. (1954). *Plenty to Watch*. New York: Viking Press.

Yashima, T., Yashima, M. & Muku, H. (1960). *The Golden Footprints*. New York: The World Publishing Company.

Teaching Idea: An Audit Trail Option

❖ Children may not be interested in participating in a comprehensive author study or teachers may find it difficult to find all of the author's books. In these situations, teachers and children may choose to make connections to other books. For example, teachers may find other books such as Mice and Beans by Ryan to discuss the similar ways the authors integrate other written languages.

In addition, children may investigate language use across genres such as poetry, biographies, autobiographies, and historical fiction. (See List of Selected Authors)

Personal Connections

Inviting children into the inquiries breaks down barriers to encourage them to take different perspectives and life associations. They do so by reflecting on their previous experiences in regard to language. One such activity that would allow for this type of investigation would be the teacher constructing a family tree during the author study to outline Yashima's family while tracing the language in the family. Children are then invited to do the same and investigate the language history in their families though family trees. They may discover that there were lost languages in the family over generations or languages added to the family because of marriage. In one such activity, a first grade Japanese-American child Emma created the following artifact.

Figure 1: Emma's Family Flower

Instead of drawing a tree, Emma decided to use a Family Flower. On the flower, Emma wrote the members of her family both in the United States and Japan. When writing her Japanese grandparents on the tree, Emma chose to write *Obaajan* (Grandmother) and *Ojii-jan* (Grandfather) in Japanese hiragana. These types of choices are cornerstones for critical discussions around why her uses in written languages paralleled Yashima's and how it created a particular type of meaning different than that of writing her Japanese grandparents in English. On the one hand, this illustrates a personal connection to her grandparents. Yet on the other hand, writing in Japanese embodies emotional and social meanings that are not always translatable. By having the right to select among written language systems, Emma was able to maintain those valuable connections that also advance her cognitive development through problem solving and decision making. In such ways, young children develop agency in making language choices, like Yashima, that best represents who they are in a complicated world in and around language.

Teaching Idea: Other Types of Activities to Engage Personal Experiences

Depending on the linguistic experiences of the children in classrooms, teachers many choose other options to bring in personal experiences. Adapted from the work of Denny Taylor (1993), the following provides a variety of options for allowing children to bring many types of familial, personal, and social connections that involve community resources.

❖ Literacy Digs. In this activity children bring in environmental print from the home and community around multiple languages.

❖ Family Interviews. Children interview family members about their experiences with multiple languages.

❖ Literacy Walks. During a literacy walk, children venture outside into the community and take pictures of environmental print that uses different languages.

❖ Family Webs. Family webs outline and trace family members and language use in the families. Children may also choose to use friends and other members not in immediate family.

Critical Literacy, Language Rights, and the Classroom

Teachers have many ways to discuss language rights in the classroom through a critical literacy approach. There are many possibilities that this approach can take and picture books are one important social milieu for integrating discussions around language and literacy in multiple languages for social justice and democratic classrooms. Picture books provide spaces where conversations and transformations can occur around multiple languages for teacher and student learning. Children recognize their multiple language identities and those of others. Additionally, we frame the use of multiple languages not through a deficit model that perpetuates inequality among linguistically diverse children, but through social and linguistic equity that allows children the multiple resources available to them to imagine and develop voices in the world around them.

Audit Trail Outline

The audit trail for the Umbrella may look something like the figure on the following page. The steps in order of appearance are numbered in each box.

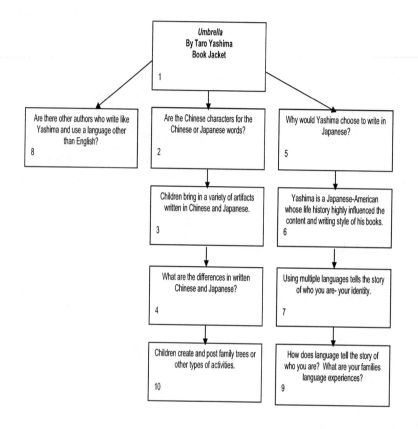

Figure 2: Audit trail outline.

Further Study

Selected Authors

African-American Literature

- Eloise Greenfield
- Patricia McKissack
- Jacqueline Woodson
- Elizabeth Fitzgerald Howard

Asian-American Literature
- Paul Kee
- Keiko Narahashi
- Yoshida Uchida
- Kim-Lan Tran

Hispanic Literature
- Authur Dorros
- Joe Hayes
- Gary Soto
- Pam Munoz Ryan
- Alma Flor Ada

Multicultural/Multilingual Book Resources

- Kaleidoscope: A multicultural booklist for Grades K-8
- The Horn Book Guide
- Scholastic Website: How to Choose the Best Multicultural Books

Researchers in Human, Language, and Literacy Rights

- Richard Ruiz
- Geneva Smitherman
- Denny Taylor

Personal Stories on Language Learning

Santa Ana, O. (Ed.). (2004). *Tongue tied: The lives of multilingual children in public education.* New York: Rowman & Littlefield.

Hoffman, E. (1989). *Lost in translation: A life in a new language.* New York: Penguin.

Fadiman, A. (1997). *The spirit catches you and you fall down: A Hmong child, her American doctors, and the collision of two cultures.* New York: Farrar, Straus & Giroux.

Rodriguez, R. (2004). *Hunger of memory: The education of Richard Rodriguez*. New York: Dial Press Trade.

Children's Books Cited

Munoz Ryan, P. (2001). *Mice and beans*. New York: Scholastic Press.

Nakagawa, H. (2006). *Sumo boy*. New York: Hyperion.

Yashima, T. (1958). *Umbrella*. New York: Viking Press.

References

Dewey, J. (1916). *Democracy and education: An introduction to the philosophy of education*. New York: The Free Press.

Dyson, A. H. (1993). *Social worlds of children learning to write in an urban primary school*. New York: Teachers College Press.

Ferreiro, E., & Teberosky, A. (1982). *Literacy before schooling*. Portsmouth: Heinemann.

Freire, P. (2003). *Pedagogy of the oppressed*. New York: Continuum.

Fu, D. (2003). *An island of English: Teaching ESL in Chinatown*. Portsmouth, NH: Heinemann.

Gale, T. (nd). *Contemporary authors*. Retrieved March 12, 2007.

Greene, M. (1995). *Releasing the imagination: Essays on education, the arts, and social change*. San Francisco, CA: Jossey-Bass.

Kabuto, B. (2006). "If I was born in the Year of the Tiger, why do I speak English?": Identity, ideology, and early biliteracy: Hofstra University.

Meek, M. (1988). *How texts teach what readers learn*. Woodchester, Great Britain: Thimble Press.

Owocki, G., & Goodman, Y. (2002). *Kidwatching: Documenting children's literacy development*. Portsmouth, NH: Heinemann.

Paley, V. G. (1997). *The girl with the brown crayon*. Cambridge, MA: Harvard University Press.

Taylor, D. (1993). *From the child's point of view*. Portsmouth, NH:

Heinemann.

Taylor, D. (2005). Resisting the new word order: Conceptualizing freedom in contradictory symbolic spaces. *Anthropology in Education Quarterly*, 36(4).

Taylor, D., & Kabuto, B. (In press). Reading everybody's child: Teaching literacy as a human right. In Y. Goodman & P. Martens (Eds.), *Critical issues in early literacy development: Research and pedagogy*: Lawrence Erlbaum.

Valdes, G. (1996). Con respeto: *Bridging the distances between culturally diverse families and schools*. New York: Teachers College Press.

Vasquez, V. (2004). *Negotiating critical literacies with young children*. Mahwah, NJ: Lawrence Erlbaum.

Whitehead, A. N. (1929). *The aims of education and other essays*. New York: The Free Press.

Wolk, S. (2004). Using picture books to teach for democracy. *Language Arts*, 82(1), 26-35

Chapter 6

Using Picture Books to Explore Cultural Messages

Susan Davis Lenski

Consider:

❖ *What age students can I use picture books with?*
❖ *What does it mean to critically examine a text?*
❖ *How does critical literacy apply to using picture books with children?*
❖ *What social issues are explored in picture books?*
❖ *Why would I use this kind of text to talk about sensitive issues?*

Picture books can be used with any age group from young children to adults to help readers explore cultural messages, identify mainstream privilege, and adopt a critical stance toward text. You can create your own list of picture books that would be conducive to teaching students in your class to read critically and to look for cultural messages. A list of books that you can use for the units that you teach throughout the year is preferable to teaching one unit or lesson on critical literacy. If you are a teacher, identify the units that you commonly teach and search for picture books that fit each topic.

As mentioned throughout this volume, it is incumbent upon teachers to critically examine books before using them and while teaching them to the students. Engage your students in the process and encourage them to become critical readers and share with them some of the criticism of the books that you are working with in class. For example, Sootface has been dismissed by Native American critics as racist and inauthentic (see www.oyate.org) and Mufaro's Beautiful Daughters has also been criticized by some who think it is completely made up and offensive. All readers can be encouraged to adopt critical stances.

If you are not teaching, select an age range that interests you, identify some topics or units that you could teach in those grades, and list a variety of books that you could use in the future. Many teachers find that listing books in a database is helpful so that they can search the list in a variety of ways. An example for intermediate grades follows.

Cinderella Stories	Civil War	Insects	Memoirs
Cendrillon: A Caribbean Cinderella	Barefoot: Escape on the Underground Railroad	Amazon Diary: Property of Alex Winters	Bigmama's
Sootface: An Ojibwa Cinderells	Follow the Drinking Gourd	Hey, Little Ant	In Coal Country
Yeh-Shen: A Cinderella Story from China	The Great Migration	Two Bad Ants	No Star Nights
Mufaro's Beautiful Daughters: An African Tale	Working Cotton	When the Woods Hum	The Potato Man

Using Picture Books to Explore Cultural Messages

Quality education encourages students to become aware of, if not actively work against, social injustice... Leonardo, 2004, p. 13.

"That's not fair," Kristin declared when she read *The Lady in the Box*, a book about a homeless woman (McGovern, 1997). Children seem to have a natural sense of fairness and a belief in social justice. Schooling, however, does not always refine those inner feelings; instead it often suppresses questioning and thinking about social issues and even discourages students from discussing issues of social justice

Children in United States classrooms are typically protected from difficult subjects (see for example other chapters in this volume from Darvin and Shannon) . Shannon (1995) writes, "schools in general and literacy programs in particular are often organized to promote a specific set of values—normal American values" (p. 15). Evan, Avery, and Pederson (1999) found that there are recognized topics that are acceptable in schools and topics, such as homelessness, that are considered taboo. The taboo topics, they found, are often the ones that are most meaningful and interesting to students.

The reasons for this protectiveness are well-intentioned. Teachers and parents want to shelter students from the harsh realities of life, especially in school curricula (Wollman-Bonilla, 1998). The texts that are used in school are most often the kind of literature that depicts "appropriate behavior" and happy endings (Boutte, 2002). In schools, therefore, children are exposed to the types of thinking and literature that promulgates the habits of mind that dismiss difficult social issues and is "disconnected from children's everyday experiences and makes classrooms appear to be places where one cannot engage in anything real or important" (Lewison, Leland, & Harste, 2000, p. 14).

These institutional beliefs leave out sensitive issues that require students to think about social injustices, the kinds of topics that are prevalent in students' lives outside of school. In reality, children are inundated with cultural messages from media, such as television, movies, and video games, that include topics that are considered inappropriate for school reading and discussion, and many children's lives are rife with circumstances that cannot be discussed at schools, such as alcohol, drug, and sexual abuse.

The Influence of Critical Literacy Theory

Critical literacy has been defined as a set of literacy practices that encourage readers to develop a critical awareness of the idea that texts represent particular points of view and omitting others (Luke & Freebody, 1997). Critical literacy is an evolving set of beliefs about a different way to approach reading.

All of the choices that an author makes—from the story outline to individual words—are influenced by the author's purposes and intentions for writing, but they are also subtly, and not so subtly, influenced by the author's humanity and language ideology as noted in Kabuto's chapter. How the author thinks about an issue or what the author feels about something can be a message of the text.

Changing the Way Teachers and Students Think

Thinking from a critical literacy perspective takes some time and experience. First, teachers need to think about ways that their own reading takes into account the social context of the author and the implications of power relations in the text. Learning how to address texts from a critical stance can be done a number of ways, one of them is through group discussions. When groups of teachers discuss their own professional readings critically, they might ask the following questions as they read and discuss:

- Who authored this text?
- What are the authors' qualifications? Do we know of any author

biases?

- What else has the author written about this topic?
- What research has the author included in the article? What has the author omitted?
- What other ways are there of thinking about this topic?
- What groups are being privileged and which groups are silenced?
- How does this text fit with other things I've read about the topic?

Teachers can also apply these same questions when hearing an educator speak.

When listening to anyone from school administrators to nationally-recognized researchers, teachers need to use critical thinking as they listen. For example, I was teaching a class in literacy leadership recently, when our university group was invited to hear Jonathan Kozol give a presentation. Before we went to the lecture, we discussed our knowledge of Kozol's books, particularly *Rachel and her Children: Homeless Families in America* (Kozol, 1988). Most of us had read the book, and we discussed how the homelessness Kozol described was similar to what we were seeing in our urban community. Our discussion centered around schooling issues such as how to teach groups of children who were highly mobile, had no school supplies, were often hungry, and had no place to read outside of school. We then went on to decry the lack of funding for schools and the cuts in social services for the homeless. We had entered a one-way discussion—we all seemed to be in agreement about the perspective of the book and the issue of homeless children.

Our group was pleased with our discussion and somewhat smug. Then I asked the teachers to approach our discussion from a critical literacy perspective. What messages were not heard and whose voices were silent in our discussion? We recognized that the perspectives of social agencies other than schools were not acknowledged nor were the legislators who had cut funding. On our journey to do what's best for children, we found ourselves guilty of being one-sided and not looking at the issue of homelessness from a perspective other than our own. From this hard lesson, we discussed ways of listening from a critical perspective. We acknowledged that we had our own biases and that these biases would be the lens from which we listened to the Kozol lecture. We agreed that we did not need to give up our world-views to be critical listeners but that critical literacy theory demands that we recognize that our individual way of thinking is just that—a worldview that is informed by our background and experiences and that shapes the way we respond to others.

Teachers, therefore, need to understand critical thinking them-selves and use it in reading and thinking before they begin to use it with their students. As teachers think about their own reading and learning from a critical stance, they begin to adapt the thinking pro-cesses in their own work. Critical thinking does not follow a template. As teachers incorporate critical literacy theory in their own lives in meaningful ways, they can begin to tailor lessons that move students' thinking towards issues of social justice.

Raising Issues of Social Justice through Picture Books

Teaching students to read critically and introducing social justice issues can take a variety of formats. One that has been quite success-ful is teaching students to read for the cultural messages of picture books. Related discussions of cultural and political messages, both implicit and explicit, are discussed in Kabuto's and Shannon's chap-ters in this book. Wolk (2004), notes that picture books can be the focal point for discussions about social justice issues and can engage children in dialogue about democracy. The value of picture books for raising issues of social justice cannot be overstated.

Even young children are capable of discussing complex issues when using books that are easy for them to read and understand (Lewis, 2001). When reading picture books with students, it is important to scaffold different levels of classroom talk as students develop their ability to think critically. Luke and Freebody (1997), for example, suggest layering questions that help students at different points in their development. Some questions for developing critical linguistic thinking are the following:

- Why do you think other students (or children) should or should not read this book?
- What questions do you have about this story?
- What surprised you about this book?
- Is there anything that bothers you about this story?
- If you were telling a friend about this story, what would you say?

Teaching Ideas:

- ❖ Write or draw a picture of a different ending for this book.
- ❖ Write or draw a picture of the main character acting differently.
- ❖ Draw a picture of a character who is not in this book but who could be.
- ❖ Draw a picture of the story taking place in a different time or place.
- ❖ Write one or two statements from someone whose perspective is represented in this book.
- ❖ Write one or two statements from someone whose perspective is not represented in this book.

After students listen to the story, they can continue to develop their critical responses by participating in writing activities that foster moving beyond the surface level of the story. Activities that encourage students to remember that the author of the book made conscious

115

and subconscious authorial choices are especially powerful. Some ideas that work with students of all ages follow:

Students of all ages respond enthusiastically to these types of activities and discussions. An example of a book that I have used is *Something Beautiful* (Wyeth, 1998). In this book, an African American girl begins noticing the homelessness and graffiti in her neighborhood. She then begins to look for "something beautiful" in all of the situations that surround her. Her new perspective inspires her to take social action by cleaning up the graffiti and trash by her home.

When reading this book with children, they immediately understand one level of cultural message from this picture book. They see how the main character was able to change her approach to her environment through actively looking for good things. Students also noticed the variety of racial groups represented in the story and how each character from the different groups was beautiful. The discussions of this book can also lead to discussions of deeper issues such as the reasons for homelessness, poverty, and racism.

Another example of using picture books with older students to explore cultural messages is *The Paper Bag Princess* (Munsch, 1980). *The Paper Bag Princess* approaches a fairy tale from a feminist perspective. When reading this book with students, they are able to enjoy the alternative view of the story: the princess rescues the prince and then rejects him because he appears to be shallow. When reading the book critically, though, the students are able to see that just as traditional fairy tales are told from the male perspective, this one is told from a female perspective—neither which is balanced. In the case of *The Paper Bag Princess*, the story is biased toward feminism, showing females as powerful and competent, and in the case of this story, depicting the male as weak. Using this picture book as an example, students are able to understand that reading critically should not just change the role of the privileged but should explore and bring to light positions of power.

Using picture books from a critical literacy perspective can also influence students' actions. After reading *Something Beautiful*, students might look for the beauty in their own worlds and look for ways to confront social injustices. Students reading *The Paper Bag Princess* might remember to look for ways society privileges either gender. In addition to changes in perspective, students can also change in their classroom relationships. In a teacher research project, Lelande, Harste, and Huber (2005) found that by reading books with children that discussed difficult social issues, the children actually were more aware of their worlds and concerned about others. In an additional finding, the researchers also found that the children were more aware of ways that they could behave with each other and solve personal problems with relationships.

Selecting Books and Topics that Foster Meaningful Discussions

Many picture books can be used to explore cultural messages; in fact, teachers can use many types of books to achieve this purpose. Harste (2000) suggests using books that explore differences among people, give voice to those who have been silenced or marginalized, show characters who engage in social action, and/or have nontraditional endings. Books that illustrate the complexity of social problems rather than ending "happily ever after" are especially appropriate. A list of recommended picture books for discussions about cultural messages can be found in Figure 1.

Picture Books for Critical Literacy Discussions

Bloom, B. (1999). *Wolf!* New York: Orchard.

Browne, A. (1986). *Piggybook.* New York: Knopf.

Bunting, E. (1991). *Fly away home.* New York: Clarion.

Cherry, L. (1992). *A river ran wild.* New York: Harcourt.

Coleman, E. (1998). *Your move.* San Diego; Harcourt Brace.

Cronin, D. (2000). *Click, clack, moo: Cows that type.* New York: Simon & Schuster.

Feiffer, J. (2001). *I'm not Bobby.* Manhasset, NY: Hyperion.

Fierstein, H. (2002). *The sissy duckling.* New York: Simon & Schuster.

Hoose, P., & Hoose, H. (1998). *Hey, little ant.* New York: Scholastic.

McGovern, A. (1997). *The lady in the box.* New York: Turtle.

Munsch, R. (1980. *The paper bag princess.* Toronto: Annick Press.

Polacco, P. (1988). *The keeping quilt.* New York: Aladdin.

Scieszka, J. (1989). *The true story of the 3 little pigs.* New York: Viking.

Wiles, D. (2001). *Freedom summer.* New York: Atheneum.

Woodson, J. (2001). *The other side.* New York: Putnam.

Woodson, J. (2002). *Visiting day.* New York: Scholastic.

Wyeth, S.D. (1998). *Something beautiful.* New York: Bantam Doubleday Dell.

Taking Action

Social justice issues can also be explored in systematic ways. Ciardiello (2004) suggests that teachers look for thematic topics around issues of social justice or human rights that are culturally relevant for the age of the students. For example, Comber (2001) describes a project for primary grade students that she used in her classroom. She decided to have her students collect junk mail and advertisements about Mother's Day. In class the students read the advertisements and drew pictures of the kinds of mothers these gifts represented. Then the students drew pictures of their mothers and the gifts that were more appropriate. By the end of the project the students realized that the advertisements were sending a message about mothers that was far from reality. From that experience, children can take action in any number of ways. For example, children can talk with their parents about realistic ways to celebrate Mother's Day; they can discuss how advertisements affect their thinking; or they can write letters to stores about the types of advertisements they promote. All of these examples show ways to move children from reading to taking action about issues in their lives.

Reading about issues of social justice is the beginning of action. For example, a young man, Craig Kielburger, read a story about child labor Pakistan. As Craig read and learned more about child labor, he became passionate about the problem and organized a movement called Kids Can Free the Children to fight for rights of children worldwide. Free the Children was begun in 1995 and was comprised of students from ages 10 through 16. The movement has grown to over 100,000 members in more than 30 countries. Craig has continued to champion the cause of child labor through Free the Children and has spoken about the issue to Congress, the Prime Minister of England, Mother Teresa, and the Pope. He has also co-authored a book titled *Free the Children: A Young Man's Personal Crusade against Child Labor* (Kielburger & Major, 1998) about his experience in moving from reading about a social issue to taking social action on a large scale.

Topics for units about social justice issues can be taken from students' lives or from readings about social issues. Students of all ages have local issues that could be used for these units. As students become more adept at thinking from a critical perspective, however, it is important that themes outside students' experiences also become topics of study. Students who have little lived experiences with poverty, for example, might read about the reasons for homelessness; and conversely, students who live in poverty can read about the very different problems of the rich. As students learn about social issues outside their existence, they become more aware of the complexities of society and learn how to think about issues of social justice.

119

Service Learning

One of the reasons that social injustices persist in our society is because we fail to "ask why things are the way they are, who benefits from these conditions, and how can we make them more equitable" (Shannon, 1995 p. 123). I am not suggesting that the use of picture books to teach cultural messages can redeem all of society, but it can certainly be one step in a very long process. What teachers do in classrooms matters.

One way teachers have used picture books to take social action is through service learning projects. Service learning projects include two main components: an activity that provides a needed service to the school, community, or agency; and learning about the project. Service learning projects are especially appropriate for extensions to reading picture books because they extend learning while taking action. An example of a service learning project that could follow reading the book Something Beautiful could be that you and your students clean up the trash around your school or the graffiti in an area near your school. The clean up is the activity. To promote learning, you could have students research the amount of trash thrown away in your locality, find out about ways trash could be used in art, or learn about the history of graffiti. Students who learn in conjunction with social action tend to become more engaged in the project and more passionate about the need for taking action. Additional service learning ideas follow.

Picture Book	Service	Learning
The Lady in the Box	Collect canned goods for homeless shelter	Research the reasons for homelessness
	Host a "canned goods" luncheon	Learn about the nutritional values of canned goods
The Paper Bag Princess	Conduct a school survey about gender inequalities	Research the history of feminism in the United States
	Volunteer to help school personnel in activities that are typically gendered. For example, have boys help serve lunch and girls assist cleaning the school.	Develop a chart that lists the teachers, staff, and support personnel in school by gender

References

Alvermann, D.E., & Hagood, M.C. (2000). Critical media literacy: Research, theory, and practice in "new times." *Journal of Educational Research*, 93, 193-205.

Apol, L. (1998). "But what does this have to do with kids?" Literary theory in children's literature in the children's literature classroom. *Journal of Children's Literature*, 24(2), 32-46.

Boutte, G.S. (2002). The critical literacy process: Guidelines for examining books. *Childhood Education*, 78, 147-152.

Cadiero-Kaplan, K. (2002). Literacy ideologies: Critically engaging the language arts curriculum. *Language Arts*, 79, 372-381.

Ciardiello, A.V. (2004). Democracy's young heroes: An instructional model of critical literacy practices. The Reading Teacher, 58, 138-147.

Comber, B. (2001). Classroom explorations in critical literacy. In H. Fehring & P. Green (Eds.), *Critical literacy: A collection of articles from the Australian Literacy Educators' Association* (pp. 90-102). Newark, DE and South Australia, Australia: International Reading Association and Australian Literacy Educators' Association.

Creighton, D.D. (19970. Critical literacy in the elementary classroom. *Language Arts*, 74, 438-445.

Damico, J., & Riddle, R.L. (2004). From answers to questions: A beginning teacher learns to teach for social justice. *Language Arts*, 82, 36-46.

Evans, R.W., Avery, P.G., & Pederson, P.V. (1999). Taboo topics: Cultural restraint on teaching social issues. *The Social Studies*, 90, 218-224.

Fairclough, N. (1989). *Power and language*. New York: Longman.

Friere, P. (1998). *Teachers as cultural workers: Letters to those who dare to teach*. Boulder, CO: Westview.

Freire, P. (1985). *The politics of education: Culture, power, and liberation.* New York: Bergin & Garvey.

Harste, J. (2000). Supporting critical conversations in classrooms. In K.M. Pierce (Ed.), *Adventuring with books: A booklist for pre-K-grade 6* (12th ed., pp. 507-554). Urbana, IL: National Council of Teachers of English.

Herbeck, J., & Beier, C. (2003). A critical literacy curriculum: Helping preservice teachers to understand reading and writing as emancipatory acts. *Thinking Classroom,* 4, 37-42.

Kielburger, C., & Major, K. (1998). *Free the children: A young man's personal crusade against child labor.* New York: HarperCollins.

Kozol, J. (1988). *Rachel and her children: Homeless families in America.* Crown: New York.

Leland, C.H., Harste, J.C., & Huber, K.R. (2005). Out of the box: Critical literacy in a first-grade classroom. *Language Arts,* 82(5), 257-268.

Leland, C.H., Harste, J., Ociepka, A., Lewison, M., & Vasquez, V. (1999). Exploring cultural literacy: You can hear a pin drop. *Language Arts,* 77(1), 70-73.

Leonardo, Z. (2004). Critical social theory and transformative knowledge: The functions of criticism in quality education. *Educational Researcher,* 33, 11-18.

Lewis, C. (2001). *Literacy practices as social acts: Power, status, and cultural norms in the classroom.* Mahwah, NJ: Lawrence Erlbaum.

Lewison, H., Leland, C., & Harste, J. (2000). "Not in my classroom!" The case for using multi-view social issues books with children. *The Australian Journal of Language and Literacy,* 23, 8-20.

Luke, A., & Freebody, P. (1997). Shaping the social practices of reading. In S. Muspratt,

A. Luke, & P. Freebody (Eds.), *Constructing critical literacies: Teaching and learning textual practice* (pp. 185-225). Cresskill, NJ: Hampton Press.

Shannon, P. (1995). *Text, lies, & videotape: Stories about life, literacy, and learning.* Portsmouth, NH: Heinemann.

Shor, I. (1999). What is critical literacy? In I. Shor & C. Pari (Eds.), *Critical literacy in action: Writing words, changing words.* Portsmouth, NH: Boynton/Cook.Press.

Wolk, S. (2004). Using picture books to teach democracy. *Language Arts*, 82, 26-35.

Wollman-Bonilla, J.E. (1998). Outrageous viewpoints: Teachers' criteria for rejecting works of children's literature. *Language Arts*, 75, 287-295.

Children's Books Cited

McGovern, A. (1997). *The lady in the box.* New York: Turtle.

Munsch, R. (1980. *The paper bag princess.* Toronto: Annick Press.

Wyeth, S.D. (1998). *Something beautiful.* New York: Bantam Doubleday Dell.

Chapter 7

Teaching for Social Justice: Using Children's Diversity Literature in Inclusive Classrooms

Renee White-Clark and Grace Lappin

Consider:

❖ *What issues are addressed in diversity education?*
❖ *Is disability a culture? Why or why not?*
❖ *What kind of classroom climate is produced by diversity literature?*

Introduction

Before you read: (A) for Agree (D) for Disagree	Statement	After you read: (A) for Agree (D) for Disagree
	Inclusion refers to the physical class placement of students with disabilities.	
	Diversity education addresses only racial and ethnic issues.	
	Classroom teachers can use literature to teach social justice.	
	Diversity literature creates a divisive classroom climate.	
	Disability is a culture.	

"As a [mainstream] White of Irish ancestry I participate fully in my cultural traditions and want to pass them on to my children. As a disabled person I also see the world from that perspective and advocate for the rights of disabled persons. Often things, even homes and sidewalks, are not built to accommodate our needs because abled persons do not see our world" (Wardle & Cruz-Janzen, 2004, p. 29).

Often, people are narrowly described by their racial and/or ethnic attributes; but all individuals are diverse in a multitude of ways because everyone belongs to a variety of different cultural groups. Many times people hear the word "diversity" and immediately decide that it only has to do with issues of race. The terms "diversity" and "multiculturalism" have been marginalized and perceived in an exclusionary fashion. But "diversity" and "multiculturalism" are very inclusive in nature and equally include other human aspects such as gender, socio-economic status, religion, language, sexual preference, and exceptionalities. Educators are advised to become culturally responsive and develop a more complete picture of their students, one which highlights the interplay of social class, gender, special needs, language, and race to effectively instruct all students in the inclusive classroom.

The current educational issue of inclusive classrooms has intensified the diversity and multiculturalism movement. Now, thirty years after PL 94-142 (IDEA) and after decades of education reform, the latest focus is the trend toward the service delivery model of full inclusion. In 2007, the U.S Department of Education reported that more than half (52.1%) of the 6 million students with disabilities, ages 6-21, were included in regular classrooms 80 percent or more of the school day in the 2004-2005 school year (U.S. Department of Education, 2007). The effective implementation of full inclusion calls for educators' acknowledgment of students' various cultural identities, including the culture of disability, that influence teaching and learning (Cushner, et al.,2006. p. 69-70). The use of children's diversity literature is a valuable tool in the inclusive classroom, encourages students' acceptance, respect, and tolerance for each other, and can be used to promote inclusion and social justice.

The Promise of Inclusion

While many educators view inclusion as an instructional construct, others perceive it as a vehicle to promote social justice. In reality, the pedagogical practices of teachers in all settings -- inclusive as well as separate settings -- can promote social justice or inequity in the classroom. As the instructional leaders, classroom teachers set the tone and establish the culture of the classroom. Educators who perceive inclusion as simply the physical and academic incorporation of students with special needs into "regular" classrooms may be unconsciously perpetuating social injustice. These teachers often possess the belief that "all children are the same" and reinforce the dominant regular education culture. Indeed, focusing on the average learner may overlook individual differences between students, and potentially harm those with exceptionalities. Students with disabilities are required to 'normalize' or 'assimilate' much like children from culturally, ethnically, socially, racially, and/or linguistically diverse backgrounds and blend into the general student population. In contrast, special educators who are able to differentiate instruction based upon the real experiences and multiple worlds of their students do a better job teaching for social justice. Freire (1998) advocated for the integration of students' real experiences into their education and supported establishing an "intimate connection" between knowledge standard to any school curriculum and knowledge based on the lived experience of the students. Teachers who are culturally responsive understand this and also understand that social interaction of equal partners in the classroom is essential to student success.

Culture of Disability

It is crucial that any dialogue about teaching for social justice include a discussion of diversity education and a brief history of disability education. The concept of diversity education evolved from the concept of cultural pluralism and has its roots in the civil rights movements of various micro-cultures (O'Connor, 1993). Culture and cultural diversity were core components of diversity education (Nieto, 1992) and now disability education. It is a reform movement with international educational and social implications. Diversity education makes cultural, ethnic, linguistic, socioeconomic differences, gender, and physical and mental disabilities a legitimate part of the social discourse (Talbani, 2003).

Disability culture cannot be defined as simply a shared experience of oppression (Gill, 1995). According to Brown (2001) persons with disabilities have forged a group identity and share a common history of oppression as well as a common bond of resilience. Persons with disabilities create examples of life and culture colored by experiences of disability; they claim their disabilities with pride as part of their identity. Brown asserts that disability culture is what has been created by persons with disabilities to describe individual life experiences rather than a way of being treated.

Brown recognizes that disability culture is not the only culture to which individuals with disabilities belong. Persons with disabilities belong to racially, ethnically, linguistically, socially, and culturally diverse groups; they are members of different countries, nationalities, religions, and professions. Disability culture varies from county to county, in various countries, and across continents. Researchers of disability studies are aware there may be fine distinctions or even larger differences but regardless of the disability or location of the person with the disability, all have encountered oppression based on their status as a person with disabilities. Considering all the possibilities of all disabilities and all cultures, Brown maintains it is probably more accurate to say that there are many cultures of disabilities.

According to Gill (1995) there are four functions of disability culture; they are, fortification, unification, communication, and recruitment. The first function, fortification defines and expresses community values and emphasizes survival over oppression; the second function, unification expresses a belief system and encourages mutual support by highlighting common values. It does not indicate heterogeneity; the third function is communication, and the purpose is to articulate to the world and each other distinction as a people through the development of art, language, symbols, and rituals. Finally, recruitment functions to celebrate difference and encourages persons with disabilities to join as part of the community; it offers a sense of belonging, and integrates disability into the individual identity. The coherence of a culture is not accomplished by members being the same or knowing the same things.

It is crucial that educators have a sound understanding of disability culture. In school settings, students with exceptionalities are often narrowly defined by their disability and not perceived as members of various other cultural groups. Currently, the nation's special education population transcends a multitude of cultural, racial, ethnic, linguistic, and socioeconomic borders. According to the U.S. Census Bureau (1998) our school aged population is indeed diverse with16 percent of school aged children coming from non-Hispanic African American backgrounds; 4 percent from non-Hispanic Asian and Pacific Islander backgrounds; 14 percent from Hispanic backgrounds; 20 percent had at least one foreign-born parent; and 5 percent were themselves foreign-born. In addition, approximately four million students with disabilities are enrolled in public elementary and secondary schools (U. S. Department of Education, Office of Civil Rights, 1995).

Teaching Idea:

Visit these Disability Culture websites:

❖ Centre for Disability Studies: University of Leeds. Available: http://www.leeds.ac.uk/disability-studies

❖ Council for Exceptional Children. Available: http://cec.sped.org/index.html

❖ Disabilities. Available: www.kidsource.com/NICHCY/literature.html

❖ Disability World Ezine. Available:http://www.disabilityworld.org/

❖ Institute on Disability Culture. Available: http://www.dimenet.com/disculture/ (text)

Diversity education

The past two decades has seen a widespread move toward incorporating the philosophy of diversity education in teacher preparation programs with the intention of increasing knowledge and sensitivity of classroom teachers towards students from diverse backgrounds.

Research from the Center for Diversity Education at the University of Washington-Seattle is clear: educational models which embrace diversity education are good for all children, not just for those from diverse backgrounds. Teachers who embrace this philosophy teach with the purpose of facilitating academic and social success for all students. Simply stated, to achieve social justice, effective educators must acknowledge the importance of all differences – social, cultural, linguistic, and cognitive differences – among their students and use this information to inform instructional decisions (Strickland, Galda, & Cullinan, 2004).

Educators who understand the principles of diversity education are culturally responsive to their students. Such educators empower their students when they take into account the "whole" child. Children are not generically viewed but perceived as individual beings; nor are all children taught to achieve one specific standard of excellence. Effective instruction is individualized and rooted to the students' background schemata. Teachers who teach for social justice understand that "there are social, cultural, and ideological conditions that shape the construction of knowledge and the development of meaning at home, in the community, and at school" (Walsh, 1991, as cited in Ramirez & Gallardo, 2001, p.7). The commitment to diversity education is best reflected through the delivery of classroom instruction honoring the overall diverse backgrounds of the students; it does not require students to reject their experiences. Instead, successful learning is, therefore, dependent on the ability of teachers to teach effectively and create culturally responsive and diverse environments.

Teaching Idea:

Visit these Diversity education websites:
- ❖ Multicultural Review. Available: www.mcreview.com
- ❖ NAME Resources (National Association for Multicultural Education). Available: www.nameorg.org
- ❖ Teaching Tolerance. Available: www.tolerance.org
- ❖ The New Advocate. Available: www.ed.arizona.edu/DE-PARTS/LRC-old/advoc.htm
- ❖ Skipping Stones. Available: www.efn.org

Children's diversity literature

In order to function as agents of social change, educators must embrace the principles of diversity education and create relevant and authentic learning episodes and establish 'communities of learners' where acceptance, critical analysis, and democracy are encouraged (Ladson-Billings, 1994). Diversity literature is a valuable strategy to initiate grand discussion, promote empathy, facilitate critical literacy, and teach the philosophy of multiculturalism in inclusive classrooms. The proper instructional use of children's diversity literature has been found to facilitate positive attitudes, acceptance, and tolerance of students. Such literature also allows students to read about characters that represent their cultures and possibly their life situations.

Similar to diversity education, children's diversity literature is often narrowly focused on the topics of racial and ethnic differences. Children's diversity literature is usually limited to books that depict characters of color, and storylines that may or may not be appropriate or even address racial issues.

Unfortunately, the selection of children's books related to special education is dated and recent publications are limited. In addition, the authors have also observed that some instructional textbooks on children's literature may only include a brief chapter or section about diversity literature providing only a cursory look at the subject with little or no focus on appropriate application.

Again, as with most children's diversity literature, the primary focus of these texts is on racial/ethnic cultures. The number of children's books that are related to special needs seems quite small. Interestingly, many of these children's literature selections are about the disabilities and not about the well-developed characters who have disabilities. Unfortunately, such literature may often be informative in nature, but lack quality literary elements such as developed storylines and plots.. It appears clear, our population of exceptional students is not receiving the benefits of diversity literature with a disability focus.

Teaching Idea:

Visit these Children's diversity literature websites:
- ❖ Celebrate Cultural Diversity through Children's Literature. Available: www.multiculturalchildrenlit.com
- ❖ Cultural Mosaics. Available: www.coe.ohiostate.edu/edtl/llc/cm.html
- ❖ Making Multicultural Connections through Trade Books. www.mcps.k12.md.us/curriculum/socialstd/MBD/Books_

Begin.

❖ Multicultural Book Review. Available: www.somedia.com/ homes/jmele/homepage.html

❖ Multicultural & International Children's Literature Links. Available: www.home.earthlink.net/-elbond/multicultural. htm

❖ Notable Books for a Global Society (International Reading Association Children's Literature & Reading Special Interest Group). Available: www.csulb.edu/org/childrens-lit

Instructional Implications

Educators' effective use of diversity literature in the classroom determines its instructional value and impact on students. Literature can be simply used as a read-aloud for aesthetic purposes, and/or to enhance students' reading comprehension. More effectively, the literary piece can be utilized as a discussion springboard to encourage students' understanding of social justice. Banks (1997) has developed a hierarchy of four curricular models for integrating diversity literature and content into the classroom. The lowest level, the *contributions approach*, involves students reading about and discussing specific cultural groups' contributions or ethnic holidays, heroes and customs. The next level, the *additive approach*, the students are exposed to literature that reflect other cultures but is taught a curricular concept without a cultural emphasis. The third level, the *transformation approach*, encourages students to view problems and themes from different cultural perspectives. The highest level, the *social approach*, challenges students to identify societal problems and apply their critical thinking skills to resolve them. This approach prompts students to perceive themselves as decision-makers, agents of change, and promoters of social justice. The following are examples of the implementation of children's diversity literature, based upon Banks' framework, into the inclusive classroom.

Lucille Clifton's (1980) storybook, *My Friend Jacob*, is narrated by an eight year-old African American boy named Sam. Sam talks about his best friend, Jacob, who is a seventeen year-old European American boy with mental retardation. Sam shares their friendship experiences and examples as to how they help and teach each other. According to Banks' framework, this selection would not be appropriate for the *contributions level* because it does not highlight a holiday or particular group of people who have made a contribution to society. At the *additive level*, the teacher would use the illustrations from this book to focus on the character with a disability who is depicted as culturally diverse. The teacher would likely use the literature to teach the concept of friendship and probably not emphasize the diversity aspects such as intellectual challenges or racial differences. The teacher would progress to the next level, *transformation*, if she/he prompted the students' understanding of acceptance along ethnic and/or disability lines. The initiation of self- reflection and class discussion about societal views toward ethnic and disability differences would escalate the teacher's instructional level to *social action*. Students would be encouraged to recognize societal injustices toward individuals with disabilities and seek avenues to provide adequate accommodations and ensure the rights of others.

Meshack Asare's (2002) book, *Sosu's Call*, is about Sosu, an African boy with a physical disability. Because he is unable to walk the villagers alienate him and he is unable to participate in community activities and unable to attend school. Sosu becomes a hero when he weathers a terrible storm by finding a drum and warning the working villagers that the village, younger children and elderly are in danger. The village later recognizes Sosu as the "brave drummer" and not just the "boy whose legs did not work". The story ends with the chief giving Sosu a shiny new wheelchair so that he can go to school with the other children.

This book would most likely be used at Banks' *additive approach*. The concepts of courage and bravery would be the teacher's primary focus of instruction while the characters' physical disability and/or his African descent in modern day life may or may not be spotlighted. The *transformation approach* would involve the teacher's discussion of the attitude and treatment of Sosu, a child with a physical disability. The teacher would elaborate the ideals of empathy and acceptance. In addition, the illustrations would rectify students' stereotypical beliefs that all people in Africa live on a safari and dress in Kente garb. The illustrator depicts the African characters as Western dressed and technologically efficient, by including a picture of a news reporter handling a video camera. At the highest level of Banks' hierarchy, the *social action approach*, the teacher could discuss the segregation of people with disabilities from a historical perspective. The teacher can further discuss civil rights of all people and past legislation, such as the American Disabilities Act (ADA) that mandates accommodations for persons with disabilities. The teacher, and students, can address the current status of this societal issue and channel their thinking toward social justice for all.

Fraustino's (2001) book, *The Hickory Chair,* tells the story of Louis, a young African American boy with blindness, and his special relationship with his grandmother. When Louis' Grandmother dies, the family gather to hear her will and learn that Gran has left a note hidden in one of her favorite things telling them what they can keep. Louis finds the notes for many of the others, but is disappointed when no one finds one for him. When the family is about to sell the rest of Grandmother's things, Louis sits in her favorite hickory chair and claims it for himself. He feels as if the missing note no longer matters because he is "on Gran's lap again," full of the memory of her love. Louis ends his story years later, when he finds the missing note in a hole in the chair's stuffing that smells of lilacs and bleach. He cherishs his memory of his grandmother's love forever.

According to Banks' hierarchy, the *contributions approach* would not be addressed. At the *additive approach* the teacher could discuss family love, relationships, family trees or generations. Even though the character is African American the story's theme of family love is universal. Louis' blindness and perception of the world could be discussed in detail because the author's vivid descriptions and rich language convey sharp images. For example, the Grandmother described Louis as her "favorite youngest grandchild with blind sight." The language evokes Louis's compensation of his senses of smell and touch, as well as his warmth of family love. At the *transformative approach* the teacher can help students understand the characters' world as a person with blindness and help youngsters imagine what it might be like to experience the world without sight. Students can learn about Braille, sight dogs, and telecommunication technology used by persons with blindness in society. The *social action approach* would again address ADA advancements to improve the quality of life for persons with disabilities and what the students, as social activists, can individually do to promote social justice.

Conclusion

Historically, students with disabilities were the ignored, undeclared, underserved, and hidden student population. The passing of the *PL 94-142*, in 1975, initiated the integration of exceptional children into "regular" classrooms to be educated in their home school districts, with their peers, in the least restrictive environments. As a result of changes occurring over the past three decades and as the model of inclusion has evolved, more and more students with special needs are being included into general education classrooms. Not only is the placement of the students in their home schools emphasized but their academic performance and socialization with same age peers is emphasized. There was a time when students with disabilities were physically "included" but socially, emotionally, and academically ignored in the general education classroom; they are now expected – and required – to be active participants in all aspects of the inclusive classroom. Diversity education requires educators, as well as other students, to acknowledge the needs, backgrounds, and culture of students with disabilities in meaningful and respectful ways.

Educators' perceptions and understanding of disability as a culture is a prerequisites for educational equity, appropriate instruction, and student success. Teachers' attitudes and knowledge of students with disabilities will impact classroom dynamics, classroom culture, and influence the learning of children with exceptionalities and their peers. The individualization of student learning and the differentiation of instruction requires teachers to recognize and address the differences children bring to school, understand that students' identities influence how they experience school, and utilize those experiences in authentic instruction (Nieto, 2004).

Diversity education is a vehicle for teachers to create inclusive classrooms that are conducive to the learning of all students in meaningful and respectful ways. Culturally responsive teachers establish learning communities where students respect each other's differences and support one another during their learning endeavors. Children's diversity literature is a valuable tool to promote class discussions and openness so that all students view their classmates as legitimate and equal peers; it is an invincible weapon against the prejudice evident within our communities and society. As Rochman (1993, p. 9) states "The best books break down borders. They surprise us - whether they are set close to home or abroad. They change our view of ourselves; they extend that phrase 'like me' to include what we thought was foreign and strange." Within the social construct of the inclusive classroom it is important for teachers to help students develop an understanding of self and others that is respectful and equitable in order to better prepare them as democratic participants in our society. Culturally responsive teachers, who implement critical literacy, can facilitate the social, emotional, and academic development of all students as active members in a democratic society and proponents of social justice and social change.

Other Resources

Self-Reflection

As educators, it is important that we constantly assess and reassess our perceptions. In this section we ask you to conduct self-reflective activities to examine your perceptions and attitudes toward diversity. Ask yourself: *How do I honestly feel? What do I believe about particular groups of people? How do these beliefs inform my teaching?* Think about how you may act differently toward specific groups of people and/or students based on your perceptions.

Assess your knowledge base about different cultural groups, including persons with disabilities. Ask yourself: *Do I really understand this culture?* Seek professional development opportunities or visit the websites in the chapter for additional resources.

Instructional Planning Reflection

As educators, it is important that we constantly assess and reassess our development. In this section we ask you to reflect on your instructional planning. Ask yourself: *Do I use children's diversity literature? How can I enrich my lessons with diverse literature?* Refer to the bibliography of children's diversity literature for possible book titles to begin working with and search for additional literature at the aforementioned websites.

Examine your lesson plans. Ask yourself: *Do I appropriately adapt materials and lessons for all learners? Do I individualize instructional content in a quality way for all students? Are materials presented in appropriate formats? To what extent do I infuse diversity into my instruction? Do I do it in a quality way respectful of all others?* Consider using children's diversity literature beyond Banks' contributions level and aim toward the ethnic additive, transformative, or social action levels.

Classroom Environment Reflection

Examine the physical environment of your classroom. Ask yourself: *How accessible is my classroom for all learners? Are materials presented in appropriate formats? Are all materials easily accessible to all students during independent work time? Is my classroom a safe and appropriate environment for all learners? Does the décor reflect the diverse nature of my changing student populations? Does my classroom represent the diversity of my students and the community?*

Examine the books in your class library to determine appropriateness and comprehensive use of children's diversity literature. Ask yourself: *Does my classroom selection represent the culture and exceptionalities of my classroom? Do I supplement the selection by adding quality literature with the changing needs of my student population?*

Evaluate the literature in your classroom. Ask yourself: *Do these books truly represent the cultural groups I am working with; do they go beyond the children represented by my classroom culture? Are the selections biased, stereotypical or disrespectful?*

Bibliography of Children's Literature (Special Needs)

Elementary- Primary

Asare, M. (2002). *Sosu's call.* La Jolla, CA: Kane/Miller Publishers. (Physical Disability)

Brown, T. (1995). *Someone special just like you.* New York, NY: Holt. (Disabilities)

Carlson, N. L. (1990). *Arnie and the new kid.* New York, NY: Penguin. (Physical Disability)

Carter, A. R. (1999). *Dustin's big school day.* Morton Grove: IL: Albert Whitman. (Down Syndrome)

Clifton, L. (1980). *My friend Jacob.* New York, NY: Penguin. (Mentally Challenged)

Fleming, V. (1993). *Be good to Eddie Lee.* New York, NY: Penguin (Down Syndrome)

Fraustino, L. R. (2001). *The hickory chair.* New York, NY: Scholastic. (Blindness)

Lears, L. (2003). *Ian's walk: A story about autism.* Morton Grove, IL: Albert Whitman. (Autism)

Liao, J. & Thomson, S. L. (2006). *The sound of colors: A journey of imagination.* London, UK: Little, Brown & Company. (Blindness)

Martin, B. Archambault, J. & Clarke, J. (1997). *Knots on a counting rope.* New York, NY: Holt. (Blindness)

Millman, I. (2000). *Moses goes to school.* New York, NY: Farrar. (Deafness)

Osofsky, A. (1995). *My Buddy.* New York, NY: Holt. (Muscular Dystrophy)

Peterson, J. W. & Ray, D. (1984). *I have a sister—My sister is deaf.* New York, NY: HarperCollins (Deafness)

Plucker, S. (2005). *Me, Hailey.* Hollidaysburg, PA: Jason & Nordic Publishers (Down Syndrome)

Polacco, P. (1998). *Thank you, Mr. Falker.* New York, NY: Penguin Young Readers Group. (Dyslexia)

Rogers, F. (2000). *Let's talk about it: Extraordinary friends.* New York, NY: Putnam. (Disability)

Schriver, M. (2001). *What's wrong with Timmy?* London, UK: Little, Brown & Company. (Disabilities)

Intermediate

Bloor, E. (1997). *Tangerine.* New York, NY: Harcourt. (Blindness)

Christopher, M., Nones, E. J. & Christopher, M. (1991). *Great quarterback switch.* London, UK: Little, Brown & Company.

(Physical Disability)

Gantos, J. (1998). *Joey Pigza swallowed the key.* New York, NY: HarperCollins (ADHD)

Hale, N. (2004). *Oh, brother: Growing up with a special needs sibling.* American Psychological Association. (Mentally Challenged)

Hamilton, V. (1983). *Sweet whispers, Brother Rush.* New York, NY: HarperCollins.(Mentally Challenged)

Kuklin, S. (2000). *Thinking big/Mine for a year: The story of a young dwarf.* New York, NY: Lothrop, Lee and Shepard. (Dwarfism)

Maguire, G. (1994). *Missing sisters.* New York, NY: Simon & Schuster. (Physical Disabilities)

Matlin, M. & Cooney, D. (2006). *Nobody's perfect.* New York, NY: Simon & Schuster. (Deafness)

McKenzie, E. K. (1990). *Stargone John.* New York, NY: Holt. (Emotional Disabilities)

McMahon, P. (2000). *Dancing wheels.* Boston, MA: Houghton Mifflin. (Physical Disabilities)

McMahon, P. (1995). *Listen for the bus: David's story.* New York, NY: Boyds Mill Press. (Blindness)

Meyer, C. (1990). *Killing the Kudu.* New York, NY: Simon & Schuster (Physical Disabilities)

Morpurgo, M. (1996). *The ghost of Grania O'Malley.* New York, NY: Viking. (Cerebral Palsy)

St. George, J. (1992). *Dear Dr. Bell....Your friend, Helen Keller.* New York, NY: Penguin. (Deafness, Blindness)

White, R. (2000). *Memories of summer.* New York, NY: Farrar. (Mental Illness)

Wolff, V. E. (2002). *Probably still Nick Swansen.* New York, NY: Simon & Schuster. (Learning Disability)

Informational

Bergman, Y. (1990). *Going places: Children living with Cerebral Palsy.* Milwaukee, WI: Gareth Steven Books. (Cerebral Palsy)

Gordon, M. A. (1999). *Let's talk about deafness.* New York, NY: Rusen Publishing Group. (Deafness)

Krementz, J. (1992). *How it feels to live with a physical disability.* New York, NY: Simon and Schuster. (Physical Disability)

Meyer, D. (1997). *Views from our shoes: Growing up with a brother or sister with special needs.* Bethesda, MD: Woodbine House. (Disabilities)

Powell, J. (1999). *Talking about disability.* Austin, TX: Raintree. (Disability)

Quinn, P. O. & Stern, J. M. (2001). *Putting on the brakes: Young people's guide to understanding Attention Deficit Hyperactivity Disorder.* American Psychological Association. (ADHD)

Sanders, P. (1992). *Let's talk about disabled people.* New York, NY: Glouster Press. (Disability)

Thomas, P. (2002). *Don't call me special: A first look at disability.* Hauppauge, NY: Barron's (Disability)

References

Asare, M. (2002). *Sosu's call.* La Jolla, CA: Kane/Miller Publishers.

Banks, J.A. (1997). *Educating citizens in a multicultural society.* New York: Teachers College Press.

Banks, J. A. & Banks, C. A. (1997). *Diversity education: Issues and perspectives (3rd edition).* Boston: Allyn and Bacon.

Banks, J. A. and McGee-Banks, C. A. (1989). *Diversity education: Issues and perspectives.* Boston: Allyn and Bacon.

Barrera, R. B., Thompson, V. D. & Dressman, M. (Eds.) (1997). *Kaleidoscope: A multicultural booklist for grades K-8 (Second edition).* Urbana, IL: National Council of Teachers of English.

Bishop, R. S. (Ed.) (1994). Kaleidoscope: *A multicultural booklist for grades K-8*. Urbana, IL: National Council of Teachers of English.

Brown, S.E. (2001). What is disability culture? *Independent Living Institute Newsletter*, 2001-12.

Center on Human Policy. *Inclusion in education: A choice for your child*. Syracuse, NY: Syracuse University. Retrieved: http://thechp.syr.edu/incdoc2b.htm.

Clifton, L. (1980). *My friend Jacob*. New York, NY: Penguin. (Mentally Challenged)

Cumming-McCann, A. (2003). Diversity education: Connecting theory to practice. *Focus on Basics: Connecting Research & Practice*, 6, B.

Cushner, K., McClelland, A. and Safford, P. (2006). *Human diversity in education: An integrative approach (Fifth edition)*. New York, NY: McGraw Hill.

Freire, P. (1998). *Pedagogy of freedom: Ethics, democracy, and civic courage*. Lanham, MD: Rowman and Littlefield.

Gill, C. J. (1995) . A psychological view of disability culture. *Disability Studies Quarterly*, Fall.

Jacobs, J. S. & Tunnell, M. O. (2004). *Children's literature, Briefly (Third edition)*. Upper Saddle River, NJ: Pearson.

Koppelman, K. L. (2005). *Understanding Human Differences: diversity education for a diverse America*. Boston: Allyn and Bacon.

Ladson-Billings, G. (1994). *The dreamkeepers: Successful teachers of African American children*. San Francisco, CA: Jossey-Bass Publishers.

McDermott, R. & Varenne, H. (1995). Culture of disability. *Anthropology and Education Quarterly*, 26, 323-348.

Nieto, S. (2004). *Affirming diversity: The sociopolitical context of diversity education (Fourth edition)*. Boston, MA: Allyn and

Bacon.

Nieto, S. (1992). *Affirming diversity: The sociopolitical context of multicultural education.* New York: Longman Publishing Co.

Norton, D. E. (2005). *Children's diversity literature: Through the eyes of many children (Second edition).* Upper Saddle River, NJ: Pearson, Merrill Prentice Hall.

O'Connor, S. (1993). *Disability and the multicultural dialogue.* Center on Human Policy, School of Education. New York: Syracuse University.

Public Law 94-142, the Education for All Handicapped Children (EAHC) Act, 1975

Public Law 107-110, the No Child Left Behind (NCLB) Act, 2001

Ramirez, L. and Gallardo, O. M. (2001). *Portraits of teachers in multicultural settings: A critical literacy approach.* Boston, MA: Allyn and Bacon.

Rochman, H. (1993). *Against borders: Promoting books for a multicultural world.* Chicago, IL: American Library Association.

Strickland, D. S., Galda, L., & Cullinan, B. E. (2004). *Language arts: Learning and teaching.* CA: Wadsworth/Thomson Learning.

Talbani, A. (2003). Keeping up appearances: Diversity education in postmodern society. *Education and Society*, 21, 5-19.

U. S. Department of Education. (2002). *Twenty-fourth annual report to Congress on the implementation of the Individuals with Disabilities Education Act.* Washington, DC: Printing Office.

U.S. Department of Education, Office of Civil Rights, (1995). Document 1995-0-396-916. http://www.ed.gov/about/offices/list/ocr/docs/hq5269.html

U. S. Census Bureau (2008). *School enrollment-Social and economic characteristics of students.* http://www.census.gov/population/www/socdemo/school/

cps2005.html

U. S. Department of Education, National Center for Education Statistics. (2007). *The condition of education 2007 (NCES 2007-064), Table 31-1.* http://nces.ed.gov/fastfacts/display. asp?id=59

U.S. Department of Education, Office of Special Education, (2008). *Children and youth with disabilities served by selected programs: 1995-2005.* http://www.census.gov/compendia/statab/tables/08s0215.xls

U. S. Census Bureau (1998). http://www.census.gov/Press-Release/www/1999/cb99-179.html

Walsh, C. (1991). *Pedagogy and the struggle for voice: Issue of language, power, and schooling for Puerto Ricans.* Westport, CT: Bergin and Garvey.

Wardle, F. and Cruz-Janzen, M. I. (2004). *Meeting the needs of multiethnic and multiracial children in schools.* Boston, MA: Allyn and Bacon.

Yokota, J. (Ed.) (2001). *Kaleidoscope: A multicultural booklist for grades K-8 (Third edition).* Urbana, IL: National Council of Teachers of English.

Chapter 8

Social Justice, Childhood, and Texts in Four (Almost) Harmonious Voices

By Kathleen, Laura, Patrick and Tim Shannon

Consider:
* ❖ *Why is a chapter about Ninja Turtles and Barbie Dolls in a book about social justice?*
* ❖ *What about being in a book about children's literature?*
* ❖ *What other texts do we encounter daily?*
* ❖ *Is it reasonable to use multimodal texts in a book about children's literature?*

This chapter discusses alternative representations or forms of text as vehicles for constructing meaning and exploring social justice issues. Television shows, film, video games, art, music and discussions surrounding toys can be considered text and as such, can be analyzed, discussed and questioned from a critical literacy perspective.

The Teenage Mutant Ninja Turtles made it impossible for Laura and Tim to disregard issues of social justice as they passed through childhood." If Kathleen and Pat turned off the Turtle's television show, Tim and Laura would turn to other Turtle texts - read their comic books, view their films or visit McDonalds to receive their figurine as the prize in a Happy Meal. Of course, the Turtles were expected to sell commodities for advertisers, but they enabled much more than that. In our household, the Turtles opened the door to issues of justice.

Laura and Tim were attracted to different aspects of the Turtles. Laura focused on the differing portrayal of males and females in the series. The Turtles (males) were active scene eaters who captured bad guys with speed and power. April O'Neil, the only female character, used her wits to outsmart some troublemakers, but she needed to be rescued often by the boys. This gender stereotype troubled Laura while watching the show. Once she obtained the figurine, Laura transformed April into a major force when Tim and Laura composed their own Turtle adventures on their bedroom floors. Tim, who is three years younger than Laura, considered violence across the shows. The Turtles were violent, and he wondered when violence was justified or could be justified. What was the difference between the martial arts of the Turtles and the "terror" of their enemies? "Why fight fighting with fighting?" he asked.

For adults who "work" with children, it's not whether issues of social justice should be considered, but how to take up issues of justice in ways that help children become more sophisticated in their thinking and actions about these matters. As our opening example demonstrates, children and youth read and design more than print in their everyday lives, and therefore, adults should think about multimodal texts for this work. In what follows, we offer three examples of working with children's texts in order to think about the world, ourselves, and others. We address three questions: With what texts do children engage and how do they read them for their own purposes? What might adults do to help children mediate those texts and complicate their understandings? and How can social theories concerning serious contemporary topics guide our work with children in times of war and injustice.

Teaching Idea:

> Pick a text (preferably a cartoon) and examine the roles it affords different genders, ages, races or other social groups. Share your analyses with your classmates or group and decide what effect a steady diet of such text might mean for children.

We approach these questions from different vantage points. Tim and Laura are graduates of a Quaker elementary school in which conflict resolution and social issues were considered frequently, but not always thoughtfully. Kathleen taught at that school and now works with preservice elementary students in an integrated Arts and Literacy Education block of courses. Pat has written about literacy and issues of social justice for the past twenty-five years. Tim and Laura are much more comfortable with multi-modal texts than are their parents. Both grasp that readers construct the meaning of texts rather than from texts and speak directly to the adult fears that children are simply dupes for what they read. Laura and Kathleen see social justice issues in every text available to children. Tim and Kathleen think that children can handle sophisticated theorizing when abstractions are placed in familiar contexts. They can, as Darvin asserts "Handle the Truth" about sensitive social justice issues when teachers provide a safe environment in which all dialogue is respected and honored.

One fear that we share from our varied experiences is that the pedagogy of social justice will become politicized in schools, determined by a partisan agenda. A politicized education amounts to no more than indoctrination, substituting one set of social stereotypes for another. What is needed for children to become politically aware is a political education that aims to teach children "how to think in ways that cultivate the capacity for judgment essential for the exercise of power and responsibilities by a democratic citizenry. It entails looking at what we normally look through, thereby making visible the otherwise unnoticed theoretical and historical forces that shape character and practices" (Euben, 1994). A political education assumes that children mediate their environment in order to make sense of it, that the mundane includes the profound, and that the exploration of the mundane is an open inquiry into the possibilities it affords for personal and social development. Childhood is the time to start political education, and schooling can provide the spaces and opportunities for children to develop as active citizens who will engage in public life and fulfill Dewey's notion that democracy must be reinvented in each generation (1916-17).

Teaching Idea:

Watch, read, or listen to popular texts about war and discuss how they might fit or not fit into the three categories of negative, mediated, or positive peace. Remember that you can choose films, video games, children's books, newspapers, comics or a host of other texts for this project.

Justice from Popular Culture - Laura

Children love popular culture, and just like adults, they use it to make sense of the power issues that surround them (Fiske,1990). To demonstrate what I mean, I could choose any aspect of popular culture from music videos to computer games to clothes and hairstyles for children or cars, sports, and home decorating for adults. I will use Mattel's Barbie for an example because of its personal charm and its nearly universal recognition. Barbie has been much maligned since its invention in the 1950s for encouraging unrealistic body standards and limited conceptions of femininity. I'll admit that I owned about twenty Barbie dolls - Barbie proper, her ethnic friends (from my parents), Skipper, Kelly, and assorted Kens (with real and plastic hair). I loved them all, and apparently I was not the only one to do so. My senior year in high school, I started a Girl's Health Collective as a space in which girls could talk about their lives at and out of school. After my first film failed to generate discussion, I used Barbie as the focus of our next meeting. All the girls wanted to talk about Barbie - how they had played with her, the awful things they had done to their dolls, and their mothers' objections to Barbie play. Students who didn't regularly frequent our meetings stopped me in the school halls to talk about their Barbie dolls. In *Barbie's Queer Accessories*, Erica Rand reported a similar experience when people found out that she was writing a book about Barbie. Rand found that women negotiated their emerging identities through their childhood Barbie play. For example, butch lesbians remembered that their Barbies were lesbian tomboys and careerist women had Barbie in executive roles during play. And of course some butch women played executive Barbie as well.

I used my Barbies to act out and expand upon the other texts in my life. I directed Barbie productions of my favorite musicals. Barbies played the parts of time traveling *Little Women*. My brother, Tim, and I started Barbie rock bands that covered Green Day and Rage Against the Machine tunes. Although Barbie was projected as a fashion doll, mine rarely bothered to dress at all. As you might imagine, my Barbies were always in the "driver's seat" in any play. In our high school feminist group, other girls described how they had cut Barbie's hair in order that she could climb trees easily and how they used Barbie's body as a canvas on which to draw. My best friend and her little sister claimed that their Barbies went on few dates in that pink Corvette, but still managed to have active sex lives with each other and Ken. For weeks, these adolescent girls who long ago passed on their Barbies to younger siblings and cousins told Barbie stories to talk about themselves in their worlds, struggling to be tomboys, lesbians, smart and or artists by using a doll which was supposed to limit their thoughts about being female. These girls from a variety of backgrounds were able to appropriate popular culture in order to explore the possibilities of their identities. They opened up what adults considered to be closed children's texts. Rand found this among women of all types who engaged during their youth in such mediation without, perhaps despite, adult intervention.

Mattel, Barbie commercials or the dolls themselves do not dictate how children play with Barbies or what they derive from that play. The manufacturers, advertisers and artifacts do not create the values that children display while playing. Children take what they find interesting or relevant about popular culture and combine it with other interesting "text" or events in their lives in order to perform their emerging identities. This is not to say that Barbie or other cultural artifacts do not embody values that can affect young minds. Barbie, for example, does seem to project a limited definition of femininity to be sure - as do shopping malls, first person shooter games and television shows. However, those definitions and the values they assume are adult representations of the world projected through popular culture. Treated as texts, children and adults can identify, name, and consider these definitions and values in order to discuss what they have to say about lives and the people who live them. As popular culture reflects those lives (and mirrors can distort reflections), it becomes a prime source for investigating issues of justice within an environment that invites children and young adults to participate. One word of caution though, be sure to provide enough space to the young in order to allow them to express their interpretations of the artifacts because they are likely to vary from the ones adults ascribe to the artifact or the young. At least, that has been my experience. Every child artifact is a text, and they all involve issues of social justice.

Teaching Idea:

Thinking about Laura's experience with Barbies, pick some text that has been criticized for its inappropriateness for children and hypothesize how you or others might use it for your own purposes. How might children find it attractive and adapt its "expected" meaning?

Many Texts to Complicate Any Issue - Kathleen

If children's texts are to help us provide a political, not a politi-cized, education, then we must acknowledge three points: 1) there are multiple interpretations of any issue--one text is never enough to make sense of a topic; 2) all texts have points of view -- question ev-ery text--Who is the author? Why was it written? What is here? What is missing?; 3) life is complicated –don't expect or accept cut and dried answers. I will use children's texts from a farm theme study to illustrate how these points can help teachers and students consider issues of social justice.

For me, the beginning of any social studies and science theme study was the gathering of texts. These included fiction and nonfic-tion across a range of reading levels that were in some way related to the theme topic. For example, farm theme books included fiction from *Harvey Potter's Balloon Farm* to *Farmer Boy* and nonfiction about farm animals, crops, and machinery, to name just a few. Be-yond books, I gathered artwork, charts, songs, figurines, and photo-graphs. A prominent sign of a theme study was the cart of "theme books" in the classroom and "theme texts" on the walls. Those books and texts were used for many purposes throughout the study. How-ever, their first purpose was as a daily, physical reminder that learning requires many texts.

During one farm theme study, I demonstrated the use of multiple texts in learning about "the bread process." Over a few days I read several nonfiction books related to bread. After reading the first text, we began a class list of the steps in the bread process that we recorded on chart paper and attached to the wall. Each time I read a new book, or section of a book, we considered what information we had already learned and what was new in this particular book. With every new text, there was new information to add to our list, as well as reorder-ing and rewording to consider. Not only did we learn about how bread was made, from the farmer sowing seeds to the consumer buying bread off a grocery story shelf, but we learned that even a book titled *From Wheat to Bread* did not include all there was to know on the topic. Authors of "bread books" wrote for many different purposes--to explain a "manufacturing" process; to consider kinds of work; to describe ways to make bread; to educate about nutrition; to tell the history of bread. In order to be active learners (and eventually active citizens), we must bring our own purposes to multiple texts written for a variety of purposes in order develop our own understanding of the topic.

As our list of the bread process developed, it was a different kind of text that led us to see what was missing from the books we read. In preparation for a trip to a local museum exhibit of Faith Ringgold's work, we read several of her books. Her work inspired us to share our learning about the bread process in the form of a quilt. The images in *Dinner at Aunt Connie's House*, made clear what was missing from our quilt and many of the books we had used for our research--people.

While most authors gave credit to a farmer for planting seeds and a baker for making bread, many people were missing from the process. Language such as, "After it's picked, trucks deliver the wheat to a large storage area called a country elevator," (Landau, 1999, p. 27) made the labor of people invisible. Our bread process quilt was a collection of machines and buildings--tractors, trucks, grain elevators, freight trains, ovens, bread-slicing machines, grocery stores, etc. The Civil Rights activists who were always present, metaphorically, at family gatherings for Dinner at Aunt Connie's House, reminded us that when we eat bread, there must always be metaphoric guests at our table as well. So we added them to our quilt--farmers, truck drivers, grain elevator operators, train engineers, bakers, delivery truck drivers, and shelf stockers. "Where are the people?" became a question to ask of every book we read. In order to see ourselves as capable of engaging in public life, we must learn that every aspect of our lives involves the physical and mental labor of people.

In a search for the people involved in the processes and products of our lives, some are easier to find than others. Usually, those with more relative power are the easiest to find. We must put extra effort into our search for the relatively powerless. That realization is critical to an effective political education. Primary grade students may not be able to articulate their understanding, but they know about power. Anyone who spends time watching children in social situations must observe that there are some who always get to choose the games and others who always follow along if they want to play at all, for example.

Although it is easier to focus on that which is apparent, teachers know it is in the best interest of our students to put the effort into searching for the powerless voices. This requires finding texts that will complicate issues for our young students in ways they can understand. For example, I used two songs to complicate the issue of farms and farming. We began the year singing "The Farmer is the Man," a song from the founding of the Grange movement, located in a Pete Seeger collection. This song places the farmer as a hero in our society, the one who "feeds us all." My students enjoyed singing the song and easily understood the farmer as the hero of the theme study. The song served as a framework from which to understand the farmer's relative power and powerlessness in our society. Many students exclaimed, "It's not fair" upon hearing a newspaper article about milk prices and the portion that goes to the farmer. Just as in the song, "the middle man's the one who gets it all."

The second song, which we learned later in the theme study, was Si Se Puede, from John McCutcheon's "Four Seasons: Autumnsongs." It was written in honor of Cesar Chavez. In order to make sense of the song, we read texts about Cesar Chavez and the lives of migrant farm workers. The texts made visible those who were invisible in the farm books we read. Several young students verbalized the questions all were intended to consider. How could farmers, who are treated unfairly by the villainous "middle men," treat laborers so unfairly? They tried to make sense of it, but in the end had to admit, "It's not fair." Heroes can be complicated.

There are no simple answers to the "conflict" among farmers, middle men, and migrant workers. Teachers should not seek simple answers. The lessons to be learned lie in realizing the complication and naming the injustice. Naming is a first step. The reading of multiple texts that represent conflicting points of view, including those of the powerful, the powerless, and those in-between, can make visible complexity and injustice in our society. Talk around multiple texts fosters values and habit of mind (Dewey's term), which can serve young citizens now and as they age. As teachers, we can use such texts to prepare our students to take an active role in our democracy, naming problems and working toward solutions that provide justice for all.

Teaching Idea:

> Take an item from your backpack. Research its production as a commodity. Discover the people who are involved in its production, packaging, delivery and sales. Speculate about their lives inside and outside of their work.

Perspectives on Violence in Children's Books – Tim

Since 9/11 and the War on Terror began, it is nearly impossible for adults and children to avoid texts about war. They flood the TV screen, newspapers, and radio airwaves as well as t-shirts, car bumpers, and "support the troops" events. Representations of war consume much of our time. For example, I watch war movies, play violent video games that simulate modern military strategies, and read books about war. As I think about my relationship with war, I realize that war's appeal is based on three central assumptions: 1) there is a definite good and a definite evil in the world, 2) good is irreconcilable with evil, and 3) the only solution is armed conflict in which good will defeat evil. In American war narratives, of course, we are good, they are evil, and our wars are justified. These assumptions make violence that should scare children and adults seem normal and necessary. Chris Hedges makes this point in *War is the Force That Gives Us Meaning*. Anyone interested in complicating war in order to promote peace must fight through these central assumptions. One way to complicate war for children is to look at many children's books that take up the subject of war and peace from differing points of view.

Although few children's books promote war, they address war and peace from many different points of view. To sort through the variations, teachers should look to theories of war and peace. In *Approaches to Peace*, David P. Barash (2000) offers two definitions of peace. He labels the first "negative peace" and defines it as "absence of war" (2). He names the second "positive peace," which is the "establishment of life-affirming and life-enhancing values and structures" (2). Experts from the Trudeau Center for Peace and Conflict Studies at the University of Toronto use these definitions to set endpoints of a continuum. Advocates of negative peace believe that conflict only takes place between sovereign powers and is irreconcilable. War can't be stopped forever; it can only be managed. According to this position, each state must use military threats and power to ensure a favorable balance of power. The midpoint of the continuum is the belief that conflict can be solved through negotiation and that maximization of military power is not the only goal. Advocates of this position teach conflict resolution and mediation. War is understood as similar to other types of personal and social conflict, and peace is negotiated. At the other end of the continuum, proponents of positive peace view conflict as a function of unequal distribution of social resources and their benefits. Accordingly, conflict arises to achieve recognition of inequalities and to redistribute resources justly. Peace then, can only be achieved through equitable redistribution of rights and benefits.

Adults interested in thinking about war and peace with their students can make good use of this continuum. In order to illustrate that point, I thought about reviewing first person shooter games, but doubted that teachers would tackle these children's texts. Instead, I spent an afternoon in a local children's library searching for books on peace and conflict. I used the three assumptions that defined war's appeal for me to sort the books along the continuum of positive and negative peace. Some books projected all three assumptions. As could be expected, there are children's books that suggest that the Americans are the good guys in the wars that they've fought. Benson Bobrick's *Fight for Freedom: The American Revolutionary War*, Patrick O'Brien's *Duel of the Ironclads*, Dianna Preston's *Remember the Lusitania*, Stephan E. Ambrose's *The Good Fight*, and the New York Time's *A Nation Challenged: A Visual History of 9/11 and Its Aftermath* all promote the "we/they" view of the world, the irreconcilable opposition of good and evil, and the inevitability of war. A steady diet of such books encourages young people to get ready to enlist in the next conflict that any president declares. I'm sure that such books are on the shelves of libraries in most nations.

I found a surprising number of books on negative peace – the absence of war. Dr. Seuss's *The Butter Battle Book*, Liz Rosenburg's *The Silence in the Mountains*, Rukhsana Khan's *The Roses in my Carpet*, Nikolai Popov's *Why?*, and Karla Kuskin's *The Upstairs Cat* each present a translation of Kuskin's last two sentences: "And nothing is dumber than war. Is that clear?" (30). Each of these books demonstrates the author's opposition to war, the third assumption, but none deny the existence of good and evil or the irreconcilability of good and evil. To use the second set of books in conjunction with the first complicates the negative definition of peace but offers few solutions other than abstinence.

Some books call for mediation. Patricia Polacco's *Pink and Say* reduces the American Civil War to a friendship between two adolescents. Michael Foreman's *War Game* and Steven Kellog's *The Island of the Skog* provide hope for peace through understanding and negotiation of differences. Through their books, these authors challenge the irreconcilability of good and evil and the inevitability of war. Setting these books on a table with all the books mentioned in the last paragraph, raises questions about the "just war" and the "absolute evil" of the "they". I found two pacifist books, which I think fall in the middle of the positive and negative peace continuum. In Munro Leaf's *The Story of Ferdinand*, a bull refuses to fight in the ring. In Umberto Eco's & Eugenio Carmi's *The Bomb and the General*, the atoms refuse to split for the generals. Pacifism, or the refusal to engage in violence, is perhaps the strongest form of mediation. Books that place this possibility in front of children increase their options when considering war or violence.

Some books reject all three basic assumptions of a "good" war story. These books complicate the definitions of good and evil. More than just providing perspective, these books suggest that there is evil in good and the possibility of good in evil. For example, Eve Bunting's *The Blue and the Gray* portrays the American Civil War as a step towards racial equality. In *Toussaint L'Ouverture: The Fight for Haiti's Freedom*, Walter Dean Myers and Jacob Lawrence describe anti-colonial revolution in Haiti, in which the Americans sided with Napoleon. In both these books, we (the United States) are both "we" and "they" in complicated stories of the overthrow of oppression. Yona Zeldis McDonough's *Peaceful Protest: The Life of Nelson Mandela* portrays the cost of non-violent efforts to bring recognition of oppressed peoples and redistribution of rights to the fore. The lives of Toussaint and Mandela complicate rebellion against oppression. Myers and Lawrence seem to justify violence for liberation. McDonough counter acts this inclination with a non-violent disruption of the regular life in a society based on oppression.

The crux of positive peace is offered in *For Every Child: The Rights of the Child in Words and Pictures* and *If the World Were a Village: A Book About the World's People.* The first book, adapted from a text by Caroline Castle, presents The United Nations' rights of children illustrated by some of the most celebrated artists of children's books. It suggests that protection of children's rights to be housed, fed, and taught are the foundation of peace in the future. David J. Smith transforms the world's population into 100 citizens who inhabit one village. It suggests that five are from the United States, that 9 speak English, that 10 are between the ages of 5 and 9, that 32 are Christian, that 60 are always hungry and 26 are severely undernourished, that 32 breathe air that's unhealthy because of pollution, that there is one teacher for all these students, that 17 can't read at all, that 20 live on less than $1 a day, that 24 have no electricity, and that there will be 200 people in this village by 2050. These facts and figures present a world based on inequality to children and offer some sense of the work to be done to bring justice for all.

Paul Fleischman's *Seedfolks* presents a way in which that work might be accomplished. Fleischman uses thirteen voices to tell one story of how a group of strangers turned a vacant lot in Cleveland into a productive garden. Young and old, Haitian, Korean, white, and Hispanic, tough, haunted, and hopeful, work together to provide a means to sustain life in a neighborhood that was experiencing decline. The book combines the mediation of the center of the continuum with the social justice of the positive end to suggest to children a productive future.

Of course, there are many other children's books that could be placed along this continuum. The point that I hope I have conveyed is that mixing these books in a library for children complicates war and violence and can complicate ideas of peace. In present day America, when war is on the front page of the paper, the bumpers of cars, the games on computers, and the lips of adults, reading and discussing these books can help children understand the complexity of war and help them think critically about their thoughts and play. Issues of war and peace, life and death are the basis of social justice.

Teaching Idea:

Talk to children about what they know about fairness. Ask them what is fair and what is unfair in their lives. Listen carefully and respond to what they say. Be sure to listen for their reasoning about fairness and unfairness without trying to improve on their reasoning or judge their responses. Let them demonstrate how they make sense of the world. Share your findings with your classmates.

Closing

We advocate a political education for children in order to help them negotiate issues of justice in their everyday lives in more sophisticated ways. We recognize that children are already engaged in these negotiations, and we understand the role of adults to be one of complicating simplistic narratives that promote politicized solutions. Toward that end, adults should acknowledge what children already know – all objects are texts that can be used to understand themselves and the world. Texts do not dictate meaning; rather readers, even young ones, mediate them for their own purposes. Political education means representation of multiple sides to any issue in which human agency is made visible, power relations are explored, and heroes are shown to be complicated people. When obvious issues of social justice are to be considered, theories explaining the issue are used to help children identify the options available to citizens.

References

Barash, D.P., ed. (2000). *Approaches to Peace: A Reader in Peace Studies*. New York: Oxford University Press.

Dewey, J. (1916-17). The need of an industrial education in an industrial democracy. *Vol. 10 Essays (1916-1917), The middle works of John Dewey*. Carbondale, IL: Southern Illinois University Press,

Euben, P. (1994). The Debate Over the Canon. *Civic Arts Review*, 9, 1, 5-21.

Fiske, J. (1990). *Understanding Popular Culture*. Boston: Unwin Hyman.

Hedges, C. (2003). *War is the Force that Gives Us Meaning*. New York: Anchor.

Rand, E. (1995). *Barbie's Queer Accessories*. Durham: Duke University Press.

Children's Literature

Ambrose, S. (2001). *The Good Fight: How World War II Was Won*. New York: Atheneum Books for Young Readers.

Bobrick, B. (2004). *Fight For Freedom: the American Revolutionary War*. New York: Atheneum Books for Young Readers.

Bunting. E. (1996). *The Blue and the Grey*. New York: Scholastic.

Castle, C. (2001). *For Every Child: The UN Convention on the Rights of the Child in words and pictures*. New York: Phyllis Fogelman Books.

Eco, U. & Carmi, E. (1989). *The Bomb and the General*. San Diego, CA: Harcourt Brace Jovanovich.

Fleischman, P. (1997). *Seedfolks*. New York: Joanna Cotler Books.

Foreman, M. (1993). *War Game*. New York: Arcade.

Kellogg, S. (1973). *The Island of the Skog*. New York: Dial Books for Young Readers.

Khan, R. (1998). *The Roses In My Carpets*. New York: Holiday

House.

Kuskin, K. (1997). *The Upstairs Cat*. New York: Clarion Books.

Landau, E. (1999). *A True Book: Wheat*. New York: Children*s Press.

Leaf, M. (1936). *The Story of Ferdinand*. New York: The Viking Press.

Levitas, M., ed. (2002). *The New York Times A Nation Challenged: A Visual History of 9/11 and its Aftermath, Young Reader's Edition*. New York: Scholastic.

McDonough, Y.Z. (2002). *Peaceful Protest: The Life of Nelson Mandela*. New York: Walker & Company

Myers, W.D. (1996). *Toussaint L'ouverture: The Fight for Haiti'sFfreedom. New York*: Simon & Schuster Books for Young Readers.

Nolen, J. (1994). *Harvey Potter's Balloon Farm*. New York: Mulberry Books.

O'Brien, P. (2003). *Duel of the Ironclads: The Monitor vs. The Virginia*. New York: Walker & Company.

Polacco, P. (1994). *Pink and Say*. New York: Philomel Books.

Popov, N. (1996). *Why?* New York: North-South Books.

Preston, D. (2003). *Remember the Lusitania!* New York: Walker & Company.

Ringgold, F. (1993). *Dinner at Aunt Connie's House*. New York: Hyperion.

Rosenberg, L. (1999). *The Silence in the Mountains*. New York: Orchard Books.

Seeger, P. (1961). *American Favorite Ballads: Tunes and Songs as Sung by Pete Seeger*. New York: Oak Publications.

Seuss, Dr. (1984). *The Butter Battle Book*. New York: Random House.

Smith, D.J. (2002). *If the World Were a Village: A Book About the World's People*. Tonawanda, NY: Kids Can Press.

Taus-Bolstad, S. (2003). *From Wheat to Bread*. Minneapolis: Lerner.

Wilder, L. (1953). *Farmer Boy*. Harper Trophy.